Life Lessons by Libby:

A Dog's Guide to Adopting and
Training Their Person

By
Libby Libbinski-Sahr
and
Laura Engel-Sahr

Stairwell Books
///

Published by Stairwell Books
9 Carleton St
Greenwich
CT 06830 USA

161 Lowther Street
York, YO31 7LZ

www.stairwellbooks.co.uk
@stairwellbooks

Life Lessons by Libby © 2020 Libby and Laura Engel-Sahr
and Stairwell Books

ISBN: 978-1-939269-78-2

PEPPERTREE
RESCUE

This book would not have been possible without the support of my companion, person, and friend Laura who served as my typist and assistant on this project. *Life Lessons by Libby: A Dog's Guide to Adopting and Training Their Person* was actually her idea. When she approached me with the concept, my initial reaction was to say: no way.

I honestly thought recalling my early days back in New York City and the trauma of being without a family or a pack would be far too difficult. Furthermore, I'd never heard of a dog writing a guidance document, let alone an entire book. Be that as it may, she hounded me until I finally agreed to embark on the project. In spite of not wanting to engage in this endeavor, and although we've been a tight cohesive unit for years, I admit that doing so has brought our entire pack even closer together.

I dedicate this book to all the homeless dogs in the world with hopes that one day they'll find the right people to adopt and train – much like I did with Bunny and Bud.

Lesson Objective and Background

My name is Libby Libbinski-Sahr and I've reigned over my household for close to fourteen years, or eighty dog years if you're a canine – which I am. You may be surprised to learn I wasn't born into royalty, but knowing how to achieve a regal title is a lesson I'm ready to share with you. Pay close attention, follow the steps in this instruction guide, and you too can learn how to become a monarch and rule over your own household.

Before I go too far, you should understand that I'm dogmatic on one central point. In an ideal world, dogs and people have a mutual understanding, respect, and appreciation for what their respective breed brings to the table. I'm aware there's an unsettling notion that dogs should be submissive to people, but it's my belief that dogs and people provide meaningful companionship and reverence for each other. If, however you're alert, astute, and assimilate the following recommendations into your life, you should be able to take this mutual respect to the next level. This is the place where *you* manage your household – your pack. This is the premise upon which the following lessons are built.

By its very nature, the title of this book, *Life Lessons by Libby: A Dog's Guide to Adopting and Training Their Person* implies that the reader, my audience, is a canis familiaris. In other words, this book is specifically aimed at teaching and inspiring everyday dogs as they navigate an unpredictable and perplexing world filled with humans.

My life has taken me from one side of the country to the other and I am now happily retired and living in a warm climate. As a dog, I've traveled far more than most people. I've seen the sights and experienced life to its fullest. I've encountered victories as well as setbacks, but the lessons I've learned along the way have made me who I am today.

Climbing to the top of the pyramid wasn't always easy, but now my people serve me, pamper me, extol my every virtue, and most of all, they adore and respect me. They bow to my every whim and obey my commands without question. I *am* the alpha female – the grand dame, the queen, the supreme ruler. Amen and hallelujah. Okay, perhaps I'm just a tiny bit delusional, but when I first came upon the people who now attend to my every need, I knew my ascension to the throne was an attainable goal. This could be you too.

Don't skip around – each step is critically important. The tips and suggestions in this guide have been proven to work. And so, let me take you back to where my story began.

My mother was a strong resolute woman – a pure-bred Pit Bull. She lived on the sixth floor of an apartment building in The Bronx (that's in New York City). Unbeknownst to her husband (not my father), she had a fleeting affair with a strapping, muscular young man, a Rhodesian Ridgeback who lived on the seventh floor in our building. She was seduced and almost mesmerized whenever his fabulous ridge became erect. She'd sneak out and visit him in seventh heaven (that's what she called the stairwell on the seventh floor) whenever her husband was taking a cat nap with the cat that lived in their apartment. The next thing she knew, a litter of puppies was born: including me. For most, this would be a joyous event and a blessing, but because her husband had been *fixed* and couldn't father puppies, he was absolutely enraged. Unfortunately, the people she lived with were also furious and disappointed with her decision to fool around on the side. There was no question that my brothers, sisters, and I were related to that man with the virile ridge who lived just one flight up from my mother.

By the time we were about six or seven weeks old, we all knew our presence was not exactly welcome. Over the course of a few days, my siblings all disappeared one by one from our apartment. They were allegedly adopted out to other families in our building, but to be honest I never saw any of them again. That left me alone with my mother, her husband, and the cat that lived with them. I'm not sure how or why the people kept me, but my life was miserable. Sure, my basic needs were met: food, water and shelter, but that was about it. My self-esteem was nonexistent and a sense of self-actualization was something that was completely off the radar.

As the months went by and I grew into a sulky teen, things became even worse. My mother loved me, even the cat loved me, but my mother's husband growled and scowled at me incessantly. He made me feel unwanted or like an irritation, something akin to a flea bite or hot spot. I hadn't done anything to him, but it was no secret he resented my very presence. I looked too much like the well-built Ridgeback on seven.

Whenever I tried to snuggle with my mother, he'd push me away with his big hairy schnoz or bark orders at me that it was time to get out and find a job. I didn't really want to leave, but remaining in such a toxic environment wasn't healthy. My mother cried when I told her I was leaving home, but she knew it was for the best. Most importantly, she told me to always be strong, resourceful, and to follow my dreams.

I waited until the people we lived with left the door ajar and then, when no one was watching, I slipped out of our apartment. It was a bold move and I was scared, but I was also hopeful a better life was waiting for me outside the confines of our building.

As you read the chapters that follow, put yourself in my paws. You are very fortunate to embark on a journey where you can study and learn my mistakes, triumphs, and life experiences.

Best wishes as you absorb the following modules in *Life Lessons by Libby: A Dog's Guide to Adopting and Training Their Person.*

Step One: Follow Your Dreams

✓ **At the end of Step One, you'll have an action plan for following your dreams.**

NOTE: If you're reading this guide, you've already acknowledged that a life of bondage and servitude is not for you or you're not particularly welcome or happy with your current living arrangements. If not, and you're satisfied being ordered to sit, stay, or rollover, I'm hopeful that this guide will open your eyes to a life that's easily attainable for most dogs.

The first step in following your dreams is to have a plan of where you want life's journey to take you. This may sound straightforward, but speaking from personal experience, it may take some deep thinking and experiencing some victories, as well as setbacks to ascertain your ultimate dream or goal.

When I first left home, I hooked up with some street-toughs, hooligans, and wayward mutts who told me about this place where lots of dog who were just starting out on their own liked to congregate. I wasn't certain whether it was a good idea to go or not, but it sounded like a fantasy. In retrospect I should have known better, but they were really persuasive and the peer pressure was just too much.

One dog, I think he was a Shorthaired Pointer, pointed me in the direction of this massive structure near East 161st Street. He told me a tall tale about hot looking guys who liked to hang out there – almost like a mecca for teenaged girls like me. Being an impressionable and gullible pup, I followed his advice and made my way to the place where I'd allegedly be welcomed with open paws. I couldn't believe following my dreams would be so simple, and much to my disappointment, it wasn't.

I arrived at the address and there were so many people milling around the entrance to the place. Perhaps they'd been sent there by the same pointer? To be completely honest, I was more than a bit clueless. I walked in between the people and scoped out the best way to enter the colossal building. I'd almost devised a plan on how to get inside, when I became overwhelmed by amazing aromas – billows of steam emanating from big shiny silver boxes on wheels parked along the outside perimeter of the place.

That's when I saw the picture of a short-haired Dachshund being held against its will in-between something that looked like a roll or bun. The hapless dog was covered in a bright yellowy goop and something that looked like thick blood. The picture was propped up on the shiny silver box: no, it was propped up on every shiny silver box, almost too graphic for my young eyes and brain to comprehend. That pointer had tricked me into going into the depths of a netherworld where they steamed Dachshunds and then ate them hot. When I realized I'd been attracted by the aroma of hot dogs, I literally vomited in the street next to one of those boxes with the picture. This wasn't a dream. This was a nightmare. But wait – it got worse.

Almost immediately after tossing my biscuits, I was ensnared in some sort of contraption with a noose-like loop at the end of a long stick and tossed head first into the back of a truck. The truck's door slammed shut behind my rear-end. I'd been kidnapped – it was like a scene out of one of those New York City police dramas on television. To make matters worse, if that's even possible, those same street-toughs, hooligans, and wayward mutts, including that pointer, who'd suggested I go to East 161st Street in the first place, had also been kidnapped and were being held in that same truck. To say I was terrified would be a gross understatement. I'd survived being barked at by my mother's husband, but this was an entirely new kind of fright.

The howling, the crying, the angry barks in the back of the truck were horrendous. The scents from so many frightened canines sent me into sensory overload. None of us could understand how or why we'd been abducted, snatched, kidnapped by the person behind the truck's steering wheel. We had no idea where we were going – and of course I had that image of the Dachshund laying on that bun with the yellow and red gunk seared into my mind. I'm not telling you this to scare you, but to serve as a warning. When following your dreams, be sure to have a well-thought-out plan in place before attempting to execute the details.

After what seemed like forever, the truck stopped and the door opened. We were each taken out one by one and processed in some sort of maximum-security penitentiary. Our paws were smeared with ink and our prints were stamped on pieces of paper. Our photos were taken: one in profile and one head-on. We each had a full physical and body search (that's too much detail for this account) followed by a bath and dip in a liquid that was supposed to remove fleas, ticks, lice, and other vermin. When this was all over, they shoved each of us into solitary confinement – a Spartan cage with a cement floor and iron bars. I could hear other dogs barking and crying nearby, but I couldn't see anyone. I was horrified, mortified, and terrified. Perhaps I blacked out at some point, but to be completely honest, I have no recollection of ever having had my rights read to me. I had no representation, no lawyer, and no counsel. This was not a dream. This was a complete nightmare.

After what seemed like a lifetime of captivity, a person came to my cell and I was escorted into a common room for an interview. Two humans, a man and woman, were there to ask me some basic questions. It was at this point I remembered my mother's advice about following my dreams, and of course my only dream was to get out of this dreadful place. Therefore, I decided to be as sweet and polite as I could. I knew that this was likely my only hope of being sprung from the hoosegow. I fluttered my eyelashes at them, kissed them, lay on my back with my paws straight up in the air, and then engaged in the obligatory wagging of my tail. This little charade continued for at least half an hour, but then my moment of salvation arrived. They ran their hands over my recently bathed head and then asked me if I wanted to go with them. I barked a single *yes*. And with that I was sprung from the big house and was out on parole. It was essentially a conditional release, but I was out of the pen, the lockup, the slammer. My dream had come true.

Sample Action Plan for Following Your Dreams

The following are examples of situations, qualities, and points to weigh when developing a plan for following your dreams. Carefully consider your responses to the following questions, and you'll soon understand your ultimate dream.

This is **not** an all-inclusive list. Your needs, desires, and dreams need to fit your lifestyle, health, and abilities.

Depending on your age and geographic location, your responses may vary from time-to-time.

1. <u>Do you like snow, ice, and/or cold weather?</u>

Yes   _____

No   _____

Unsure   _____

If yes, a home at a ski resort may be best for you. Your DNA may prove that you're descended from a Siberian Husky, Bernese Mountain Dog, or St. Bernard.

If no, attempt to adopt a family that lives in a warm weather location. You may be part Greyhound or Beagle, or like me, you may simply prefer a balmy sunny day to sub-zero blizzard-like winds and temperatures.

2. <u>Do you like rain or getting wet?</u>

Yes   _____

No   _____

Unsure   _____

If yes, a family with a boat or a beach house may be suitable for you. You may also want to apply for a job as a hair or fur washer at one of those fancy schmancy doggy salons.

If no, perhaps a home in the desert is best for you. Take my advice: try not to get dirty. The cleaner you are, the less likely you'll need to be bathed, showered, or dunked.

3. <u>Do you enjoy the company of other dogs? Cats? Other four-legged beings?</u>

Yes   _____
No   _____
Unsure   _____

If yes, you should consider adopting a veterinarian or farmer. You may want to consider going to school to become a veterinarian, zoologist, or mammologist.

If no, adopt someone who is ready to turn their home over to you unconditionally. It's best you hang out with your people, and your people's people. That'll be sure all attention is focused on you.

4. <u>Do you prefer to be a leader or a follower?</u>

Leader   _____
Follower   _____
Unsure   _____

If you are a leader, it is vital that you train your people as soon as possible after adoption. This is *not* the time to be submissive or complacent.

Speak up and make sure your wants, needs, and desires are clearly understood by those around you.

If you are a follower, just go with the flow and perhaps things will work out for you one day. Perhaps you'll be happy – and perhaps you won't. Perhaps you'll be lucky enough to sleep in a soft, warm, cozy bed – or perhaps you won't. Good luck to you

5. <u>Do you enjoy being coerced into fetching a stick, ball, or other inanimate object?</u>

Yes   _____

No   _____

Unsure   _____

If yes, you should consider a career on the stage or in a circus. Be your own person!

If no, I applaud you and your sense of self-worth. You're someone who knows that chasing an inanimate object – molded out of some sort of synthetic material, is nothing more than an outlandish way to amuse others. Don't stoop to their level. Maintain your dignity.

Step Two: Choose Your Person Carefully

✓ **At the end of Step Two, you'll understand the significance of selecting the appropriate person(s) for adoption.**

NOTE: Adopting the correct person is absolutely critical and may be the most important decision of your life. If you select someone who is incompatible with you and your personal preferences, then achieving your dream may be an impossibility. Worse yet, be careful not to adopt a person who attempts to be your superior. Nothing good can ever come from this kind of arrangement.

Exercise extreme caution when interviewing a person for potential adoption. If you're fortunate, the adoption process may be managed by an unbiased agency that specializes in screening people to be sure they're well-suited for you, your personality, and your dreams. Even so, you may want to submit them to your own personal test and weigh their reaction to one of your behaviors. (I'll share that technique later in this chapter.)

In the previous lesson, I discussed following one's dreams, but this included victories, as well as setbacks. Always keep in mind that your goals will likely evolve over time. Your ultimate objective as a young pup will likely be far different than your objective as a senior citizen. As an example, some pups just want to hook-up with other dogs by hanging out at a special fire hydrant, light pole, or tree. Others enjoy sniffing out and chasing chipmunks, squirrels, or rabbits that have infiltrated their property; while many dogs take boundless pleasure from inhaling the sweet fragrances emitted by another dog's derrière. On the other paw, many seniors, such as me, simply relish lying in the sun or embracing their person under an oversized blanket. Whatever your age or preference, be certain to adopt a person who (1) either shares your passion for whatever you enjoy most or (2) encourages you to follow your own passion and be an independent thinker.

Remember: be vigilant and think things through. My initial goal was to find that alleged nirvana at East 161st Street where young dogs like me were welcomed with no questions asked – and yet by the time I was a hardened convict in the lock-up, my only desire was to be paroled and restart my life.

🐕 🐕 🐕 🐕 🐕

21

And so – back to that man and woman who posted my bail. I'd never seen them before and to be brutally honest, I wasn't entirely certain they could be trusted, but my options were severely limited. Who were they and what did they want? Why did they spend the time and money to get me out of that place and where were they taking me? It was all very puzzling, troubling, and nerve-wracking. Perhaps they were bail bondsmen and they simply wanted to set me loose somewhere, and then put on their hats as dog bounty hunters. Or even worse, perhaps they were taking me to the same horrific place where that wretched Dachshund had its picture taken with the yellow and red goop on the bun.

I'm not ashamed to say I was more than a bit anxious when I got into the back of their car. First of all, they didn't know me and I didn't know them. They insisted I ride in the back seat inside this big hunky plastic box with holes drilled for air and a flimsy aluminum door. It was a cage, not a prison cell, but it was far too confining for my taste. A week or so earlier being forced into that contraption would have been thoroughly humiliating, but after what I endured while in the big house, this was a walk in the park. Plus, there was a big fluffy blanket inside the box which I took as a positive sign of things to come. As I sat inside the box in the backseat of the car, I took a deep breath and told myself to hope for the best, but to plan for the worst.

It seemed as if we'd been traveling forever and I really needed to stretch my legs. I wasn't certain how to give them the signal, so I started blowing some super stinky farts and pretty soon they pulled off the highway at a rest area. The woman opened the door to my confined space and attached a leash to me. I suppose she wanted me to guide her around outside the car. It was at this point that I started to have some of my questions answered. She was very calm, patient, and told me to take my time as I squatted with my tail straight out behind me. It felt great to relieve myself in a place other than a jail cell. She even stood by while I then kicked up some dirt to cover my deposit – even though she then carefully took a bag from her pocket and proceeded to pick up what I'd dumped on the ground. I thought she wanted to preserve it as a special keepsake of our trip, which would have been wonderful, but then she immediately tossed it into a rusty garbage dumpster near the car. I was totally baffled by her behavior. Even though I wanted to like her, a voice whispered into my subconsciousness that perhaps she was a serial killer who collected gruesome souvenirs from her prey!

While I was squatting near the car, the man had walked into the building near our parking spot. He soon emerged with a bag that secreted a delightful fragrance. He reached in the bag, pulled something out, and carefully unwrapped it. I then watched as he opened his mouth as wide as he could and take a bite out of the item – and then another. It looked incredible and the smell was absolutely intoxicating. Obviously, the treat was for him and not for me, but I made it abundantly clear that I wanted to partake in whatever it was he was eating. I emitted a moaning sound, the type that people generally associate with yearning for something just out of reach: which the food obviously was. The man looked at me, broke off a tiny piece of the item, and then handed it to me. Sure, his offering was small, but it's the thought that counts. And so, after our short rest just off the highway, we all returned to our assigned seats in the car: the man and woman in the front and me in the back-seat cage. At this point, I figured they were my new family and things might be okay, but I was way off base.

After a couple more hours, we finally arrived at our destination. I'd managed to fall asleep for a while, but being cooped up wasn't exactly conducive to a peaceful rest. I really needed some serious REM sleep. We all exited the car and I was immediately struck at how quiet it was – plus the fact that there was so much grass and too many trees to count. I'd never been in such a place and I knew we weren't in The Bronx anymore. I had a feeling we were now somewhere in upstate New York. They gave me a brief moment to sniff one of the trees and I instantly knew I wasn't the only dog in the neighborhood. In fact, I could tell that several dogs, most of which I couldn't clearly identify, had left their calling cards on or near that tree. I thought I recognized the faint fragrance of a female Pit Bull, which made me think of my mother, but I wasn't one-hundred percent certain. Of course, that made me a tad homesick for The Bronx – not the big house, but my old apartment and I would have welcomed a trip down memory lane. Regrettably I didn't have time to lay in the grass to reminisce, because I was promptly guided into a nearby building.

Much to my delight, once inside I was welcomed with open paws. I initially thought this was my new home, but I quickly learned that this was a place where dogs and cats were taken for physical and psychological evaluations, as well as some down time – a chance to decompress and reset their thought processes. Perhaps they wanted to be certain I was in tip top shape and my social-emotional skills were well developed. I was undeniably dumbfounded when the man and woman left me there. I thought we'd developed a relationship, an understanding, a sense of family, but no: they dumped me at that place all by myself. Don't worry, it wasn't as bad as it sounds. The people were amazingly nice and hospitable. It wasn't anything like being a prisoner in the hoosegow. If anything, I'd gone from one extreme to the other in just a matter of hours.

First, I was treated to a warm sudsy bath, shampooed and conditioned: not like the harsh institutional soap that was unceremoniously doused onto my body in prison, but with the type of high-end beauty products they only peddle on television. That would have been great, but then I had a professional comb-out, a facial, a manicure, a pedicure with an exfoliation treatment, a spritz of perfume, followed by my first ever full-body massage. To be honest, I thought I had died and this was heaven. No – really! I sincerely thought I was a dead dog and I'd arrived at the big doggy salon in the sky.

Since I'm writing this, it's obvious that I was still very much alive. After the beauty treatment, a woman examined me and – much to my bewilderment – gave me a few injections. The exam was superficial, but being assaulted with a needle and inoculated with who knows what, caught me by surprise after being treated so well in the salon.

Following the visit to the beauty parlor and the unwarranted assault, I was led into a big room where several other dogs were milling about. It was a bit perplexing trying to sniff each other. Every dog smelled the same: a combination of the shampoo, conditioner, and perfume that was used in the other room. We shared our respective tales of how we'd come to be in that place. One dog in particular, an elderly Dachshund, almost passed out when I told my story of what I'd witnessed outside that place at East 161st Street. That night we all slept together. That poor Dachshund cried most of night, which made me feel awful, so I tried to reassure him that we were nowhere near that horrendous place. I wasn't sure if this was it, my new home or whether this was just another step on my life's journey.

As I mentioned at the beginning of this lesson, adopting the correct person(s) is absolutely critical.

The next morning, my big moment finally arrived. I was taken in a van to an exclusive boutique where special supplies, such as food, beds, treats, and beauty accessories, are sold for dogs and cats. I think the store was an establishment that only caters to pets that are deemed smart and deserving of only the best in life. As soon as I got out of the van, I was excited to see the man and woman who'd posted my bail at the jail. They took turns gently scratching behind my ears and I hypothesized that since I'd been bathed and successfully screened, both psychologically and physiologically, they'd now take me home with them. I would have been very happy going with them, but I soon learned the truth. They weren't *my* man and woman – they were only my chaperones, my escorts, my bodyguards.

I was ready to go shopping inside the boutique, but instead we loitered outside on the sidewalk in front of the place. Complete strangers started coming over to us and I could see them talking to the man and woman while everyone looked at me. It was at that point, I realized I was there to interview a person for my adoption. This was my big moment: my time to shine. I knew it was critical that I exercise extreme caution and to only select people who could be trained and taught to care for me in the manner I so richly deserved. So far, my entire life had been miserable – an unwanted and unwelcomed child, kicked out into the streets, hoodwinked by thugs, arrested and tossed into the clink, poked, prodded, harassed – well you know the story. I wanted people, I needed people who would not only care for my physical needs, but would also care for my psychological needs and emotional needs. I'm not ashamed to say it, but after what I'd experienced, I had some emotional baggage that demanded attention. I needed people who would encourage me to realize my full potential, to explore my independent side and my creative side. It was crucial that I find someone who would crown me queen.

The weather was nice that day, but I was getting tired of being on display for the people who stopped by to ask about me. It was like being a piece of pottery in a museum: they looked at me from different angles, some took photos (and no, I never signed a release for such things), and others just smiled and pointed at me. Actually, I was exhausted and really needed some down time. There was an open cage, similar to the one I traveled in a couple of days earlier sitting nearby.

And so, I strolled inside, curled up, and fell soundly asleep. That's when my life changed.

At first, I thought I was dreaming and I'd soon wake up to the harsh reality that no one even wanted to submit to my interview and exclusive screening process, but as the afternoon wore on a couple walked up and I could hear them talking with my chaperones. I listened from inside the cage as they all chatted. I opened one eye and could see a kindly looking man and woman peering inside the cage at me. They looked nice enough, the tone of their voices sounded calm, but would they live up to *my* standards – that was my number one concern. As soon as our gazes intersected, that was it.

Before I knew what had happened, my chaperones, the man and woman, and I all walked inside the boutique together. Unbeknownst to me, and I might add without consulting me, the couple had decided to allow me to adopt them. I never even had an opportunity to ask them any questions or peruse their resume, so instead I quickly needed to devise a plan "B". Rather than an interview, I knew they needed to be tested to be certain they were sincere and trustworthy.

My test (and I highly recommend this test) was to gauge their reaction to my relieving my bladder inside the boutique. This test is really quite straightforward and is graded on a simple pass–fail basis. If they are disturbed, perturbed, and angered by such a move, then they are not sincere and may displace or dump you at a moment's notice. In other words, this would constitute a failing grade. On the other paw, if they simply reach for the nearest cleaning supplies to wipe the floor while expressing a slightly worried smile or uttering a nervous laugh, then these are people who can be trusted and trained. They passed without hesitation.

<u>NOTE</u>: A failing grade is a mandatory reason for *not* adopting someone.

Almost as soon as we entered the building, I initiated the test and the people passed with flying colors. Not only did they pass, but while inside the boutique they insisted on purchasing only the best food available, new ceramic bowls in which to serve my meals, a snazzy new turquoise collar and matching leash, a queen-size canine bed with a memory foam mattress, the latest model in pooper-scoopers, and some high-end treats – the ones that are individually wrapped and only displayed near the cash register. After making their purchases and cleaning up my pee on the floor, the people signed the adoption papers – and they were mine. After all I'd been through, I finally had my own people.

From that moment forward, my life has never been the same. Remember: this could be you too! Review the checklist on the following page for tips and ideas on how to adopt the correct person(s).

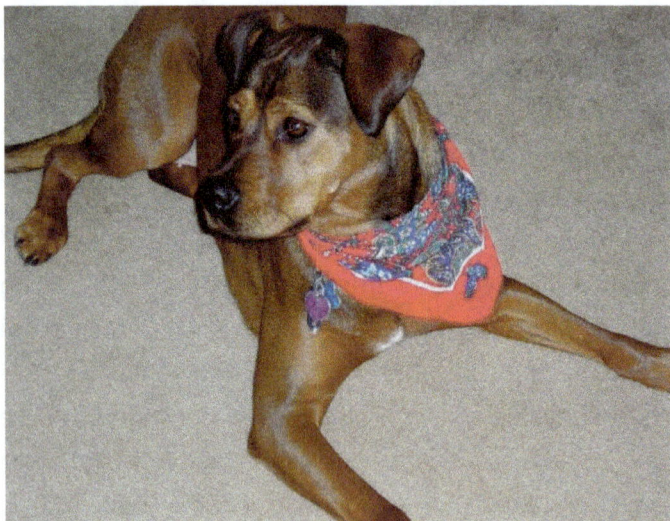

1. **Do you want to adopt a person who is ready to dedicate their entire life to yours?**

Yes   _____
No   _____
Unsure   _____

If yes, exercise extreme caution to be certain your chosen person is trainable. Communication is the key. Don't be reluctant to let your thoughts be known.

If no, why on earth not? For far too long, dogs have been subservient to people. This is your time to step up and be the leader you were born to be.

2. **Do you care if your person gets annoyed or upset with you?**

Yes   _____
No   _____
Unsure   _____

If yes, you want to live in perfect harmony with your person. You try to avoid conflict. This may mean a little give and take in your relationship, but be careful not to fall into the trap of being submissive to others in your pack.

If no, you either have no empathy or have been exposed to far too many harsh situations. You need to be your own dog and appreciate your own sense of right and wrong. Don't be the fall guy, a chump, a scapegoat for what others may have done.

3. Is it more important that you please your person or that your person pleases you?

Please my person   _____
Person pleases me   _____
Unsure   _____

If you answered *please my person*, you need therapy and likely answered *no* to question #1.

If you answered *person pleases me*, you're a smart dog who knows what they want in life.

4. Do you believe dogs should be subservient to their people or equals aka peers?

Subservient   _____
Equals   _____
Unsure   _____

If you responded *subservient*, you definitely need to work on your self-esteem. You may want to consider a period of self-reflection, counseling, or analysis. Your feelings – your emotions – are just as important as anyone else's. Don't let anyone tell you otherwise.

If you responded *equals*, you know that dogs and people are both animals with feelings. You applaud your sense of worth and laudable self-esteem. We should meet for lunch sometime to share our respective strategies and stories.

5. <u>Did you submit your people to the test explained in this lesson and did they pass?</u>

Yes	_____
No	_____
Unsure	_____

If yes, you've picked the correct people and you can now work to achieve your dreams.

If no, do **not** go home with those people – better to wait for the right people to come along.

Step Three: The Training Process Should Start Immediately

✓ **At the end of Step Three, you'll understand the critical importance of commencing the training process as soon as possible after adopting your person.**

NOTE: Even if you truly believe you've made the correct decision in adopting your person(s), a trial period is essential. The trial period is the ideal time to (1) ensure they're ready to devote their last dying breath to you, (2) will bow to your every whim, and (3) treat you like royalty. It is vital to start training your people during this time. In other words, this is akin to an audition. If you were casting a flashy musical, you want to be sure the lead can hit the high notes with ease, learn and execute the choreography, and encompasses the right chemistry with others in the cast. Do NOT skip this step.

By now, you've learned about following your dream and how to select the right people who'll serve and care for you. It's not uncommon to initially misjudge the two-legged beings who express an interest in opening their home to four-legged strangers. Humans are perplexing beings and, unlike dogs, they can't always be trusted. As you likely know, dogs are not afraid to show their feelings, their likes and dislikes, their fears and reservations, their desire for things such as a piece of juicy steak, a slice of turkey, or a beautiful bone.

In contrast, humans have been known to smile, laugh, and spend time with others, while at the same time absolutely despising their very presence. They pretend to like others, all the while wishing they would drop off the face of the earth into the pits of a raging inferno. I've even heard of people who adopt puppies as gifts and when they grow into mature dogs, they give them the old dumperoosky. Now, this is wrong on many different levels. First: a dog is not synonymous with a coffee maker, a pair of socks, or a piece of jewelry. We are living, breathing beings with wants, needs, and emotions. We aren't inanimate objects that can be purchased as gifts and returned if it's the wrong size or doesn't fit in with a specific decor. We're not a novelty, a fad, or a status symbol to be displayed as if we're a vase or piece of art. The very notion that someone could bring a canine child into their home and then send it back as if it's the wrong color, or maybe barks, is too sad for words. People speak – dogs bark. How and why people don't understand that concept is beyond me. Speaking as a dog, to think that we shouldn't bark, howl, or even woof on occasion is both cruel and crazy.

Second: dogs make a special effort to bond with their people. The humans in our lives are our pack. To break that bond for no rational reason other than they (1) only wanted a puppy and not a dog (don't get me started on that concept), or (2) decided to move to a place that doesn't accept dogs (don't get me started on that either), or (3) the dog may shed their fur – which is totally out of a dog's control, is just plain wrong. I'm aware that there are occasions when humans agonize over the fact that they are too ill to care for their canine, and in those cases I can only hope that the dog is able to select a new home and pack where they'll be welcomed and loved.

I know this all sounds frightening and rather peculiar, but believe me – it happens much more than you can imagine. I'm not certain why people aren't as open and honest as dogs, but they aren't. That's a fact and there's nothing dogs can do to modify their behavior. That's why choosing the right person for adoption and engaging in a thorough trial period is vital. I strongly advise that the trial period commence concurrently with the training process. By launching their training in sync with their trial or audition, you should have a clear understanding of whether or not they're a good fit for you within a day or two. Remember: this method has been proven to work for the vast majority of dogs (see disclaimer below).[1]

[1] A few dogs have failed to pick up on the signs they adopted an incompatible person, but failure is rare. In those rare instances, the failure rate has been highest amongst inbred dogs – those whose father was also their uncle, brother, or nephew. If this fits your description, I am truly sorry.

Now let me take you back to running the test: peeing on the floor in the pet boutique after the people had signed the adoption papers. Before leaving the store, I bid a fond and grateful farewell to the couple who'd posted my bail and escorted me away from my former life, to what I hoped would be a life of love and luxury.

I was no longer just the daughter of the Pit Bull and Ridgeback from The Bronx – no, I was on the threshold of a brand-new existence where I hoped to be free to blossom, learn new skills, and most important, train my people to serve me.

And so, I happily hopped into the back seat of their car and we headed for my new home. I was nervous, but had a good feeling about things to come. Actually, I think the people were a bit nervous too. They kept talking to each other and looking at me as we traveled from the boutique to *our* house. Perhaps they were discussing their plans for pampering their new pooch or, I suppose they could have been reliving the test I administered on the floor of the store. To be completely honest, I'm not sure what they were saying, but it really didn't matter. I'd adopted them and they now belonged to me. For ease of describing my new life, I'll refer to them as Bunny and Bud.

As soon as we returned home, they placed my new snazzy collar around my neck. As a special surprise, while we were still in the store, Bunny had made a charm for me. It was absolutely stunning and I was so incredibly moved, I wanted to cry. The charm was a bright shiny red heart. On one side it read "Libby" and on the other side was Bunny and Bud's name, address, and phone number. It was the first personal and truly meaningful gift I'd ever received. Yes, they bought the bed and treats for me, but this had my name and their name together and it made me feel verklempt – overcome with emotion. I remember that moment as if it were yesterday.

Even with my new pendant around my neck, I was a bit concerned that our first night together would be a challenge. I needed to stand my ground, train them with a firm paw, and never let them forget I was in charge. Okay – perhaps I may have been a little bit cocky that first day, thinking I knew all there was to know. What I quickly realized was that there were actually a few life lessons I hadn't yet learned.

Our first meal together was a prime example of my unfamiliarity of how a true queen should live. They planned a great homecoming/adoption celebration menu with some sort of meat cooked outside on the grill. Everything smelled wonderful, but I'd never really tasted that kind of food. I mean: my food had always come from a plain paper sack or was scooped out of a tin can. Sure, I loved the enticing aroma of their food, but I'd never really had an occasion to taste, savor, or sample what people ate. This isn't to say I didn't want to partake of something other than the hard kibble or goopy slop with clear gel on top; I'd just never had the opportunity and I sure didn't want to risk my status in the house by asking for a bite. I know some dogs loiter nearby while people eat and wait for something to hit the floor, and that's their treat. I'm not really certain why they do this or how they could stoop so low as to eat second-hand food from a dirty floor. No – I was content to eat the food that was presented in my new bowl and then sit and watch while Bunny and Bud dined on their celebratory meal.

Boy oh boy did I have a lot to learn. They sat at the table, I sat on the other side of the room, and that's when it happened. Bunny leaned down and set a plate full of food on the floor. It wasn't gunk from a can. It was my very own cheeseburger: cooked to perfection and topped with a thick slice of cheddar, carefully cut into bite sized pieces, with a generous serving of impeccably seasoned rice pilaf accompanied by steamed carrots with a hint of melted butter and light brown sugar. I was dumbfounded and wasn't certain whether (1) this was a trick or a test, or (2) I was actually hallucinating, or (3) these people were going to treat me as an equal – or better yet, their queen. If this was a trick or test to assess my self-control I sure didn't want to flunk. If the plate of food was a mirage, it was pretty darn convincing, and if they were planning to make me their peer or ruler, I was more than ready to accept.

My hunch was that it was definitely a test. And so, I didn't move an inch toward the plate for fear I'd fail and get voted out of the house. They'd snuff out my torch and ship me back to my humble beginnings in the clink. As I stared at the food and inhaled the savory smells, I had the sensation that drool was starting to trickle from my tongue onto the floor. Bud then pushed the plate closer to me and pointed to the food. I took this as a signal that perhaps it wasn't a trick, a test, or a hallucination. Still, this was uncharted territory and I didn't want to blow my chance at joining their pack. As a dog, my canine instinct was to slobber down every last piece on the plate as quickly as possible, but my cultivated and coherent side implored me to cool my jets and sit tight. I mustered all of my self-control and ran through the various scenarios in my head. I finally settled on the notion that perhaps they truly brought me into their home as an equal partner, an associate, or a colleague. Of course, I didn't want to be rude, so I made the decision to eat the food. The taste exceeded my wildest expectations. The meat was a picture-perfect medium rare with a slightly charred flavor, the rice was soft and fluffy, the carrots were cooked through – but not mushy. From that moment, it was clear that dinner would be a time to share food, discuss our respective days, and to enjoy each other's company. Meals will be discussed in-depth in additional lessons.

After our first dinner together, I decided to take my people for a walk around my new neighborhood, and then it was time for bed. I was dog-tired and looked forward to my first night in my new home. Based on what I'd experienced thus far, at this point I was actually ready to forego the trial period for assessing our mutual compatibility, but then things took an unexpected turn.

Following what was an exceptional evening: a delicious dinner, a wonderful walk, a bit of television time, Bunny guided me to a corner of their living room and there was a big metal pen with my new bed inside. Needless to say, I was beyond shocked. Not only was I shocked, I was hurt – not physically, but emotionally. Why she wanted to lock me up was a genuine mystery. Up to this point, I honestly thought we were starting to bond, have a woman-to-woman understanding, a feeling of trust and mutual admiration, but then she pushed my bottom, my tuchus, my behind into the crate and locked the door. Well I was doggone dumbfounded. Perhaps the plate of food had been a trick and I was going to be returned, like a collar that didn't fit or a bag of food that had bugs or was past its recommended "best if used by" date. She turned off the lights and then disappeared up the stairs, leaving me alone in the dark. Sure, I had my new bed but this was just plain wrong. A friend doesn't lock up their friend, a host doesn't shut out their guest, and a servant certainly doesn't lock up their monarch. It was imperative that I clarify our respective roles sooner rather than later, and let it be known that I was not going to sleep alone in a downstairs corner while they slept together elsewhere in the house.

This is when I knew I needed to initiate another test for them, to assess whether or not they'd successfully pass a trial period. It was time to grab the gusto and let it all out. It was time to break the glass and sound the alarm. I started to cry, to howl, to bark, to whine – not from physical pain, but from emotional pain. I pulled out all the stops and let my unleashed emotions flow. My goal was to see (1) if Bunny or Bud would call out to me from wherever they were in the house, (2) ignore me altogether and let me suffer and cry alone in the dark, or (3) come downstairs and release me from my unwarranted and unjustified confinement. Not only did they pass my test by freeing me from this embarrassing isolation, but I was invited upstairs to their room.

That night, they placed my new bed on the floor next to their bed and that's where it remained. That simple act of kindness demonstrated their trial period had been successfully completed and I was ready to finalize the adoption of my people. The delicious food, their realization that a terrible mistake had been made by forcing me into a cage, my beautiful new pendant – it was all coming together. My dreams, my goals, my desire to live life to the fullest, to adopt people who would serve me, love me, and care for me were coming true. Sure, there was still work to do and adventures to come, but I knew I was on the right track to a happy life.

Training your person and observing their behaviors during a trial period can be awkward. Exercise caution. The key to succeeding during this stage of your relationship is to walk a fine line between being a total pushover or dejected wimp and being overly assertive or forceful and displaying your alpha side. As a newbie in the house, you don't want to overstep yourself. Save demonstrations of confidence and assertiveness for later in this process.

At this point in your relationship, I strongly recommend providing and receiving exhibitions of gratitude and love. On the providing side of things, don't be afraid to kiss your person. If they don't appreciate kisses and other demonstrations of affection, they'll let you know. Why anyone wouldn't welcome a canoodle from their canine is beyond me, but be that as it may, some people just don't. In contrast, some of those same people may kiss their dogs without hesitation. I know your reflex may be to pull away when human lips enter your personal space, but you should make every effort to receive their exhibition of love with a sense of charm and grace. Kissing and hugging are primarily behaviors that humans (aka homo sapiens) and apes (aka hominoidea) display. Just go along with it and humor them. It's an instinctual behavior that helps them bond.

Review the checklist on the following page for tips and ideas on how to train the correct person(s).

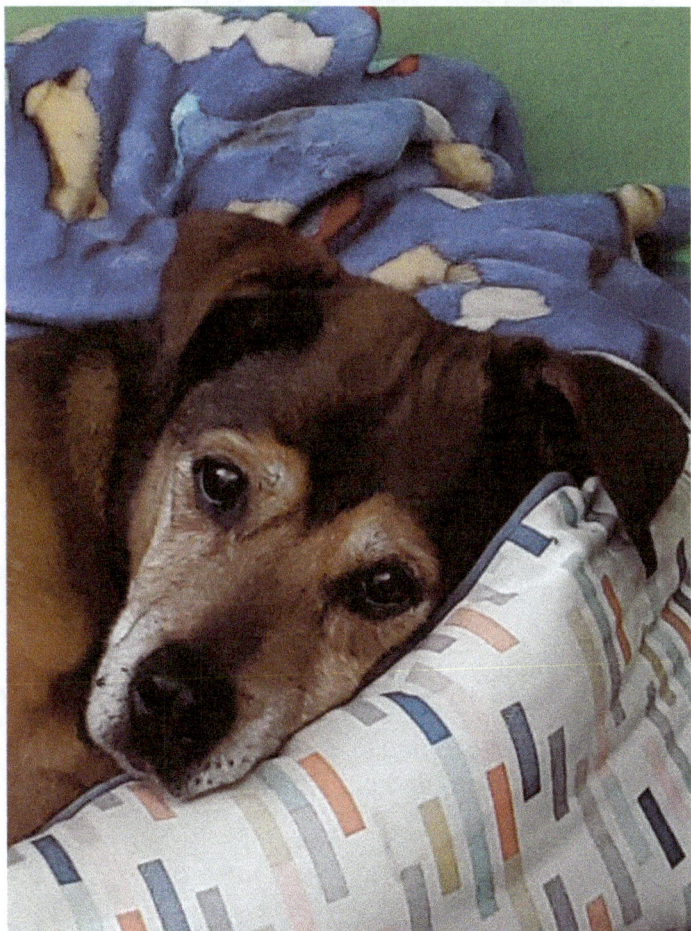

1. <u>Did your person purchase a pendant or charm engraved with your name?</u>

Yes   _____

No   _____

Unsure   _____

If yes, they obviously like you. If not, they wouldn't have spent the money on jewelry.

If no, don't get comfortable. They may return you, but don't despair. Things could improve.

2. <u>Were you served a delicious hot meal or a bowl of cold gruel on your first night?</u>

Hot meal   _____

Cold gruel   _____

Unsure   _____

If hot meal, you've made a good choice. Play their games and you'll never go hungry.

If cold gruel, perhaps they're just a bit confused. Give them time and perhaps they'll learn.

3. Did you offer to take your person on a walk – and did they accept?

Yes   _____
No   _____
Unsure   _____

If yes, be certain to locate a conspicuous place on your neighbor's lawn to pee and poop.

If no, try again. Don't give up – keep trying. They may have been too tired on day one.

4. On night one, did you sleep alone in the dark or in the same room as your new pack?

Dark room alone   _____
Same room as people   _____
Unsure   _____

If you were forced to sleep alone, reassess your situation. This is a bad sign for the future. If you slept in the same room, you're definitely in the right place and with right people.

51

5.   <u>Did you kiss your person?</u>

Yes   _____
No   _____

If yes, I applaud your willingness to display and share your emotions with the person who just put themselves in your paws and welcomed you into their home.

If no, why not? If you tried and were rejected, I recommend trying again in a couple of weeks. Don't feel bad. Some people just don't appreciate a juicy canine kiss.

6. <u>Did your person kiss you?</u>

Yes   _____
No   _____

If yes, you're a daring dog to allow a person to kiss you so early in the relationship. Developing a sense of trust between you and your new pack is vital and your acceptance of their kiss is a positive sign of things to come.

If no, don't fret. Your people may be shy or hesitant to kiss you without knowing you a bit better. A kiss may still come when you least expect it. Be patient.

Step Four: Don't be Shy -Taking the Next Step

✓ **At the end of Step Four, you'll appreciate the importance of communicating your wants and needs, likes and dislikes, enjoyments and fears.**

NOTE: By now, you and your people have likely started to settle into a routine. Remember – don't be complacent. You still have work to do to cement your place in the pecking-order of the household. They're probably still treating you like a newcomer. It's time to start molding their hearts and minds to ensure you're placed on the proverbial pedestal to be loved, adored, and honored.

Training your person is not a straightforward or effortless process. In fact, it is imperative to treat this as a lifelong project – one that's never truly complete. Think of their training as an evolutionary progression with ever-changing goals based solely on *your* personal needs and desires. This lesson is divided into two topics which are the backbone of the training process: (1) Bedtime and Sleeping and (2) Dining Options.

Remember, your people are not mind readers or psychics. If you don't tell them what you want, don't get upset when they fail to produce results. This is not the time to be shy, but there's no need to be overly raucous either. In other words, don't start barking or howling like a dog and expect them to respond in a positive manner. Such overt vocal displays could actually result in the opposite outcome. I know this is a harsh truth, but not all people appreciate a barking dog. Obviously, those types often possess negative biases against canines, and they should have been weeded-out during the screening and interview process. If, however you somehow landed in a place living with such a human: only use unconcealed audio exhibitions in extreme circumstances.

Bed Time and Sleeping

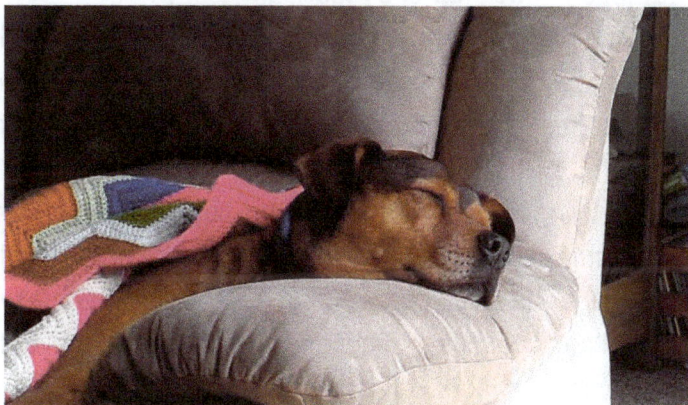

The following provides an overview of Bunny and Bud's evolutionary progression with regards to understanding, accepting, and enabling our respective sleeping arrangements.

That first night started off a bit rough, but as soon as I let it be known that my bed and I belonged in the same room as theirs, things quickly improved. The central point is that I communicated my annoyance at the very notion that *I* should sleep alone. After conveying my thoughts, they placed my new memory foam bed on the floor in their room. That was okay for a while – and for you it may be all you want. When you think about it, a soft cushy bed is a nice perk for many dogs. Then again, if you believe you're destined to be a queen, much more is required.

One night while my people were sleeping, I noticed there was a queen-sized quilt folded up on a chair in the corner of the bedroom. The chair certainly didn't need it and Bunny and Bud hadn't used it since I'd been living with them, so I gently pulled it onto the floor and curled up inside the folded layers of luxury and warmth. The following morning, they smiled when they saw I'd made myself a nest of sorts: perfectly molded to my royal shape. So as not to disturb my handiwork, they made the respectful decision to leave it in place for the following night, and the following night, and so forth. Okay, that was a step in the right direction. I now essentially had two beds with one on either side of the room, but a bed needs a pillow or two and a blanket. And so, I helped myself to one of their pillows and shortly thereafter, Bunny bought me a beautiful baby blue blanket and a second pillow. It was now perfectly clear that my wants and needs were being understood by those I'd chosen to serve me.

At this point, most dogs would have been quite content with their sleeping arrangements – but *I'm* not most dogs. In fact, two beds with all of the accoutrements would be fine for the vast majority of canines. On the other paw, for those of us (and if you're reading this guide, I'm including you in this category) who only want the best in life, there was only one more step that needed to be taken. I needed to sleep in their bed.

Bud and I had really started to bond. Sure, I was also getting along with Bunny, but I needed to start my ascension to being the alpha female in the family. Since Bunny and I were the only two females in the house, I knew I needed to convince Bud that I was his chosen one – his favorite. You may think achieving this goal was a complicated task, and yet it was really much simpler than it sounds.

Most nights, Bud went upstairs much earlier than Bunny and me. She and I'd stay downstairs and watch movies or news programs together. At precisely 8:30 every evening, I'd stand and stare at her just long enough to grab her attention and then stroll over to the back door. That was her signal that it was time to escort me to my toileting facility in their backyard. After coming back inside, she'd gently wipe all four paws with a plush towel and then get me undressed by removing my collar, the one with the pendant. That was my signal that bedtime was fast approaching. In contrast, Bud generally watched television in bed and for some unknown reason, he liked to watch big sweaty men chasing, kicking, or throwing different types of balls. He particularly enjoyed watching men hit a small ball with a big wooden stick after which they'd run like crazy. I made every effort to grasp the point of the exercise, but couldn't understand why they were running so fast when it seemed they only ended up right back where they started in the first place. In my opinion, it would only be worth exerting so much energy if there was something really good to eat waiting for me at the end, perhaps a rack of ribs or some barbequed chicken with a side of mac and cheese. Of course, what he watched is actually irrelevant to my instructions. What *is* relevant however, was that fact that he always fell asleep while watching. After weighing the positives and negatives and studying Bunny and Bud's respective sleep schedules, I developed a plan.

One night after I did my business in the backyard, I went straight upstairs while she opted to stay down for a while. Unlike most evenings, I purposely told her I needed to go out a bit earlier than. I had a hunch she wouldn't go to bed quite yet – and that was all part of the strategy. Bunny was obviously oblivious to my overall objective. After getting undressed, I quickly ascended the stairs to our bedroom where, as usual, Bud was fast asleep with the television still playing. Instead of getting into either my bed or nest, I quickly hopped up on the bed and laid down next to Bud with my head on Bunny's pillows. It was perfect. I was in bed with him and she was nowhere in sight. I'm not certain whether or not he was conscious, but he quietly said goodnight and then turned off the television, all without opening his eyes. It was incredible! I'd never in all my years felt so secure, or loved.

I must have fallen asleep right away because the next thing I knew, Bunny was also trying to get into the same bed. I could hear her grumbling under her breath and feel her fingers in my back as she tried to move me. At this point, I was wide awake although I did my best to pretend to be asleep. Their bed is far bigger than mine, but for three of us to squeeze in together was just a bit too tight for me. Bud and I were fine sleeping together, and I certainly didn't need *her* joining us. And then my big moment arrived: Bud mumbled something in his sleep and Bunny stormed out of the room. Turned out she slept in one of their guest rooms that night, while Bud and I embraced each other in peaceful slumber. I was the alpha female, at least for that night. The following nights, I was able to cuddle in bed with Bud, but when *she* was ready to sleep, I was given the boot. Okay: not really a boot, but I was asked to sleep in one of my own beds. I suppose it was a reasonable compromise.

The lesson is a straightforward one. Inform your person where and how you want to sleep, with what types of linens, and with whom. Change takes time and even I started out with the humblest of beginnings. However by planning the proper course of action and adopting people who desperately wanted to please me, they developed a thorough understanding of who was actually in charge. I don't sleep with my man Bud every night, but fortunately Bunny occasionally goes out-of-town for work – and then he's all mine.

Review the checklist on the following page to ascertain your style of sleeping arrangements.

1. <u>Are you satisfied sleeping on the floor or do you prefer a bed?</u>

Floor   _____

Bed   _____

Unsure   _____

If you're satisfied sleeping on the floor, then you obviously have much to learn.

If you prefer a bed, you're a smart pup who knows what they want.

2. <u>Assuming you prefer a bed, do you like one pillow or two?</u>

One   _____

Two   _____

None   _____

If you prefer one pillow, be certain it's a soft and pliable one.

If you prefer two pillows, you're like me – one for my head and one for my tush.

If you don't need a pillow, then you obviously have much to learn.

3. <u>Do you like to sleep alone or do you prefer to sleep with others?</u>

Alone   _____

Others   _____

Unsure   _____

If you prefer to sleep alone, perhaps you should seek the expertise of a sleep specialist.

If you prefer to sleep with others, you have likely already ascended the hierarchal scale.

4. <u>Assuming you prefer sleeping with others, do you prefer one or two others with you?</u>

One   _____

Two   _____

Unsure   _____

If you prefer one person, you've likely selected your preferred person in the house.

If you prefer to sleep with two people, you may want to consider a career as an escort.

Dining Options

For many dogs, meal times are highlights in their day. Now, I'm not claiming to be a nutritionist, a culinary critic, or food quality expert – although I do have an educated palate and an appreciation for the finer foods most canines enjoy. I will eat most anything and I am an ardent omnivore. On the other paw, I am most definitely not a cannibal and the very notion of eating a Dachshund on a bun or anything that is referred to as a *hot dog* is both offensive and revolting to my sense of decorum and dignity. To do so would be akin to a swine eating a pig in a blanket, a bovine eating a cowboy steak, or a cat eating catsup (that's just a doggy joke).

Needless to say, it's taken many years and careful training to reach this pinnacle of doggy dining proficiency. Remember: if you don't tell your people what you want, don't get upset when they fail to produce results. This may come as a shock, but many people will only do the bare minimum in life in order to get a passing grade. In other words, they may purchase generic, bland, and tasteless nourishment for you – and by doing so, they get credit for feeding you, but that's about it. The big question you need to ask yourself is: do you eat simply to remain alive, or do you eat food to excite your taste buds, for the enjoyment, for the overall dining experience? As with most other things, your dining preferences are an evolutionary process.

Following our meal on our first night together, things progressed quite nicely. You should know I'm not a dog food snob. In fact, there are really quite a few high-end products manufactured for dogs of taste. My point is that you shouldn't be lulled into thinking you should only eat what your people are eating. By not sampling the varied options specifically crafted for a dog's taste, people are the ones who are truly missing out. Personally, I enjoy both moist and dry cuisines prepared explicitly for dogs. Don't laugh – there are some fine culinary canine treats that I sincerely believe Bunny and Bud would appreciate, but are reluctant to sample. The following are some of my favorite dinner choices: braised duck breast served with sautéed spinach and wild rice; slow simmered beef stew with sliced carrots, russet potatoes, and French-cut green beans; and roast turkey and gravy served with candied yams and baby peas. On the snack side of things, I prefer all varieties of peanut butter treats or an all-natural raw hide chew with a delicately pounded and dried chicken breast carefully wrapped around the outside. Now, I know you must be salivating right now, as am I just by disclosing these descriptions, and yet it baffles me as to why my people don't share in these delights.

Where you eat is just as important as what you eat. I recall when I first adopted my people, for some odd reason they opted to serve my dry food in a genuine faux china bowl in the foyer near the front door. Yes: my moist cuisine was served in the kitchen, but not my dry food. The only thing I can think of is that perhaps they were geographically challenged or unhinged or oblivious to do such a thing. I wanted to eat near their big sliding door at the back of the house. That way I could eat and watch the squirrels, birds, and the occasional deer or fox while dining. It was like dinner and a show. And so, every day Bunny would set the dry food down before leaving for work and every day I'd pick up the filled bowl in my superbly robust jaw and carry it through the house to my desired location. You may be shocked to learn that although Bunny is reasonably intelligent, it took her at least a week before she finally got the hint and placed my bowl at the back door instead of the front door. Perhaps she needed a new light bulb over her head or a reboot in her internal computer. I had confidence that sooner or later, she'd get the hint and correct her error. Why it took more than a single day is still baffling, but she obviously required some special coaching from me to get the bowl placement correct.

This isn't to say I don't appreciate the same food my people eat. If you're only dining on food manufactured and marketed to dogs, it may be time to broaden your gastronomic horizons. You may be thinking, how do I do this if my people aren't quite as generous as Bunny and Bud? The answer is really quite simple: just help yourself when they're not looking. Trust me, even though I'm generally invited to share in their dinner, there have been occasions when I wasn't offered what was being prepared and/or served in their kitchen.

Early on in our relationship, I recall two specific occasions when I wanted to wolf down food that wasn't being served to me. The first time was an oversized corn muffin – sliced in two with gobs of sweet butter slathered on each half. It looked perfect and the pastry's color reminded me of a golden retriever. For some unknown reason, Bud prepared the treat, but then needed to leave the house for a while. There it was, just sitting on the kitchen counter. The paper cup used for baking the goody had been conveniently removed, the topping applied, and no one was around to enjoy it. The freshly baked pastry looked so forlorn – so lost. And so, I hopped up on my back paws and propped my front paws on the edge of the counter immediately adjacent to the deserted muffin. To reach over with my full set of canine teeth and grab the tasty treat was quick and easy: no fuss, no muss. Even I surprised myself by managing to secure the entire item in my mouth while leaving the ceramic plate in place. It was truly a skillful move, if I must say so myself. I have fond and delicious memories of that conquest. In retrospect, I should have taken the time to savor each buttery bite, but it was gone within a matter of moments. The only evidence that proved the muffin had ever existed was the empty plate and some corn muffin crumbs on the floor. I suppose I could have licked those up, but what kind of dog eats food off the floor? Certainly not me!

The second occasion occurred not long thereafter. Even by my standards, it was an incredibly bold move and I can still remember the flavors as if it were yesterday. Bunny had purchased a special treat at a local bake shop: a peach praline pie. She and Bud each had a small taste without so much as offering me a sample size snack. I could see they enjoyed the pie and why I wasn't included was a mystery, but suffice it to say, I wasn't invited to the table. Whether it was intentional or an oversight is of no importance. What is noteworthy however, is that I wasn't provided a piece, an incredibly selfish act on their part, and now I wanted it more than ever. The pie, minus two inconsequential slices, was covered in foil and placed on the kitchen counter, pushed back from the edge. They must have thought that (1) unlike the golden retriever colored corn muffin it was out of sight and reach of my skillful paws or (2) there was no possible way for me to help myself to their treat. I waited until they left the house and then I made my move. I mustered every bit of strength I had and then I leapt up onto the kitchen counter. As I stood upon the Formica surface, I surveyed other treats that had previously been out of reach. Sure, there were a few boxes of crackers, but the foil-covered delight was what I'd come for and it was important to stay on task. It did occur to me that I could probably reach the freezer from there and retrieve the ice cream, which would be a nice accompaniment to the pie, but the logistics in opening the freezer, locating the ice cream, and then safely returning to the floor would have required an in-depth strategic plan.

And so, I grabbed the pie plate in my teeth and then jumped down onto the floor. So far – so good. I peeled back the covering, left it on the kitchen floor, and then took the pie plate into the living room. Yes, I could have eaten it in the kitchen, but such a delicacy required a change of venue. Up to this point, I'd dined on many foods cooked for Bunny and Bud's table, but nothing prepared me for this. Unlike my escapade with the corn muffin, I took my time and savored each juicy bite. The pie crust was so flaky and buttery and the candied pecans on top were to die for. When my taste buds encountered the filling, I almost fell into a trance. The sweet, juicy, peach filling had a hint of cinnamon and it just about sent me into a total state of bliss. I'd never encountered such flavors – such luxury. For a brief moment I reconsidered my plan to add the ice cream to the pie, but to do so would have been far too complicated, plus the pie was calling out to me. *Eat me – love me – treasure me.* It was a moment to remember. After eating the top crust, I lapped up the fruit filling and then the bottom crust. Finally, I licked the entire pie plate clean. Every last bit of crust and perfectly baked peach filling now rested inside my very full stomach. The entire peach praline pie affair was both invigorating and exhausting. I strolled over to my water dish in the kitchen for a tall cool beverage and then went upstairs to Bunny and Bud's bed for a little siesta.

My gastronomic adventures in the kitchen did upset my people, but they got over it soon enough. Their love and admiration for my athletic skills in procuring the corn muffin and the pie outweighed any negative thoughts they may have had. Actually, they started including me more frequently in their journeys to explore local dining favorites. For some reason, dogs are often excluded from most dining establishments.

Not only is this overt discrimination, but it is hurtful and just plain rude. Fortunately for all parties concerned, we located some restaurants that welcomed canine customers and their people. Regrettably, these places mandate that dogs like me dine outside[2]. Also, the climate in upstate New York only provides a limited number of months each year when outside dining is possible, but that was still okay. It was the thought that counted most. I quickly developed three preferred places to go out to eat.

My favorite was a place in Saratoga Springs that served barbequed chicken and ribs. Not only did they welcome dogs, but they provided a special location for their doggy diners. I always indulged in the charbroiled chicken coated in a sweet barbeque sauce, carefully boned and presented by Bunny on a paper plate. Whenever we'd dine there, we'd sit in the exclusive high-end section reserved for dogs and their people. I suppose dog-less customers could have booked a table in that area, but to be brutally honest, they would have looked totally out of place.

---

[2] I am not a *service* dog, which means I'm not welcome in most establishments. On the other hand, I do appreciate being serviced and cared for by my service people.

Another one of my haunts was a restaurant in Halfmoon, New York where I usually ordered the half-pound cheeseburger (plain - with no pickle, tomato, or mayo) and a side of freshly made crinkle-cut french fries. Okay: perhaps I only ate a couple of fries, but I also enjoyed a soft vanilla cone for dessert. Regrettably I always wanted the medium sized cone (cake cone, rather than sugar cone), but for some unknown reason Bunny and Bud would only purchase the kiddie-sized one for me.

The last place I must mention is a restaurant I only had an opportunity to visit once, but it was truly memorable. It was a steakhouse/sidewalk café located on Church Street in Burlington, Vermont – only a few blocks from Lake Champlain. If I recall correctly, my people ordered the petite sirloin for me (cooked rare) with a side of mashed potatoes. Sure, the waiter seemed a bit perplexed when Bunny told the waiter what I wanted to order and how I wanted it prepared, but he brought my meal out from the kitchen with everyone else's food just the same. I'm not certain why, but the manager of the establishment did insist on serving my food on a disposable plate rather than china – which was more than a bit offensive, but I wasn't about to complain. I was just happy to be included. Well – the taste was exquisite: a hint of salt, pepper, and garlic on the meat's charred exterior. Following our dinner, we walked down the street and purchased some locally made all-natural vanilla ice cream from Ben and Jerry's. It was a delightful evening.

And so, as you can clearly see my people and I evolved together from eating at home, perhaps with a simple can of dog food or a burger, to ordering off the menu in an upscale restaurant. Don't be shy in letting your dining requests be known. Not all dogs are quite as brazen as I am, however I'm confident you'll discover your comfort zone with regards to food.

Review the following checklist to ascertain your style of dining.

1. If you had your choice, would you opt for canned food or fresh food?

Canned	_____
Fresh	_____
Unsure	_____

If you selected canned food, then you clearly have much to learn.

If you prefer fresh food, I recommend only selecting organic ingredients.

2. Would you eat food off the floor – aka scraps, seconds, crumbs?

Yes	_____
No	_____
Unsure	_____

If you answered yes, you need to work on your self-esteem. You're better than this.

If you answered no, I admire your strength and confidence.

3. Do you prefer to order your meat rare, medium, or well-done?

Rare   _____

Medium   _____

Well Done   _____

If you prefer rare, congratulations! You're still in touch with your deep Canis roots.

If you prefer to medium, that's okay too, but you should try rare though. It's more flavorful.

If you prefer well-done, you may need help and should reconnect with your genetic self.

4. When dining in a restaurant, is it permissible to place your paws on the table?

Yes   _____

No   _____

Unsure   _____

If you answered yes, be sure to only eat in places with plastic utensils.

If you answered no, you've obviously had the good fortune to dine in finer establishments.

Step Five: Your Family is *Your* Pack

✓ **At the end of Step Five, you'll understand that you are part of a family and that your family is your pack.**

NOTE: At this stage of your training, you've already established yourself as a full-fledged member of the household. Although your people may appear to be ready to serve you, you should realize that they have feelings too. Like you, they may have ups and downs, emotional baggage, likes and dislikes, etc. Treat your people – your humans – as you would have them treat you.

As soon as we were introduced, we all had an undeniable emotional connection. Theoretically, my people could have opted to adopt a purebred Beagle, Border Collie, or Basset Hound with an unadulterated pedigree and papers to prove their lineage. Instead, they went out on a limb and decided to allow the illegitimate daughter of a pit bull and ridgeback to move in with them. Not only was I not some unblemished thoroughbred, I'd been arrested and incarcerated prior to coming into their lives. Now that I'm entrenched in their lives, I realize their move took tremendous courage. I'm no longer the paroled mutt searching for a dream in the streets of The Bronx. I'm now living the dream and caring for my people.

My family, my pack, my humans are primarily Bunny and Bud, however our pack extends far beyond the three of us. It encompasses other people and countless canine companions. Now and then I reflect on my behaviors as a youth. It's horrifying to think that I purposely peed in the boutique and then absconded with the peach praline pie. As I write this guide filled with my life lessons, you must realize that I've mellowed and matured. In years past, I was primarily focused on my own thoughts and feelings, but I now realize my constant companionship and love is genuinely important to the mutual wellbeing of our entire pack.

If you can believe it, when I first met my people, they were hesitant to kiss me or even confide in me. Perhaps they wanted to be sure we were all compatible, possessed comparable political and religious beliefs, and enjoyed similar types of cuisine before becoming emotionally attached. Fortunately for them, they soon learned that I could keep secrets and I was always ready with a kiss and a hug. The confidential conversations I overheard and/or took part in … well obviously I can't share those.

I suppose what I'm trying to say is that many dogs, such as me – and perhaps even you – often moonlight as amateur therapists or psychologists. In this role, our primary task is to sit and listen with a nonjudgmental ear. We may feel the need to offer recommendations, words of encouragement, or even chastisement (depending on the topic at hand), but it's really best to keep those thoughts to yourself. If you believe you absolutely must offer advice, just stop and put yourself in their paws. How would you feel if you just needed a sounding board – someone who would listen without passing judgement – and then they suddenly starting barking their thoughts at you? I know I wouldn't be too happy. And so remember, sometimes just having a canine companion to talk to is enough to help your people through a difficult situation.

When I think back to the day I adopted my family, I'm ashamed to admit that I didn't always consider their feelings. Obviously, it was their decision to come to the adoption clinic, but in retrospect, I should have realized there was a reason they chose to attend that day. There was no way for me to have known that they'd brought another dog into their lives many years earlier: a gentle and emotionally scarred Black Lab-Shepherd mix named Snowball. I've since learned that she too had been in the lock-up, not in New York City, but in a place known as Menands. Her's was an incredibly sad story, but suffice it to say, Snowball was unceremoniously imprisoned by her own people. I know it's shocking, but there are people who, for one reason or another, do such things. I can only hope it was because they were simply unable to care for her, but there she was in the clink. Like me, it was a lucky day when Snowball, Bunny, and Bud encountered each other.

When I saw photos of her prominently displayed in their house, as well as a small memorial to her – complete with her collar and personalized pendant – I should have understood how much she meant to them. From what I now understand, she died at a very old age just a few months prior to our meeting at the boutique. I imagine they treated her much like they treat me, but I knew I wasn't a replacement for Snowball. No – I was just another lucky dog to be adopted by this loving family. Knowing I was not the first dog to be part of this pack and to live in this house actually gave me a sense of comfort. Even though I didn't always show it, I knew these were people who purposely sought out dogs who were down on their luck, dogs who truly needed a loving home and shoulder to cry on. As the years have progressed however, I now know people often need dog's shoulders to cry on too.

When I chose Bunny and Bud so many years ago, I suppose I was just a tad immature. Perhaps our shared life experiences helped teach me benevolence, boosted my emotional intelligence and overall emotional quotient. Whenever I've felt just a bit under the weather or not up to par, they've always taken such good care of me. I recall several instances when I felt more like an underdog than a queen, and yet they always managed to bring me out of my funk. On one occasion when I had a sore immediately adjacent to my bottom (I'm not going to discuss the dirty details), they treated me with utmost love. Suffice it to say, my doctor instructed Bunny (Bud was suddenly unavailable) to hot pack the region located immediately underneath the start of my tail. When she held that hot, damp washcloth on my sore and sensitive flesh, it felt wonderful. I still recall how nervous she was, but when Bunny realized how the steaming wet compress soothed my physical, and might I add, my emotional needs, she was happy and honored to help. Tending to my tender tush was an intimate time for both of us.

Now that I think about it, they've always gone out of their way to assist me – especially when I was placed in uncomfortable and incredibly embarrassing situations. I'll never forget this sad, but true tale. Try not to get too squeamish or alarmed when you hear what happened.

I had some sort of tiny growth on one of my wrists, or perhaps it was an ankle. Anyway, my doctor removed it with no problems and no complications. I was happy. She was happy. My people were happy, but then for no apparent or rational reason my doctor attached a crazy contraption around my neck. The inexplicable apparatus was a gigantic hunk of plastic in the shape of a cone with a putrid pink ribbon woven along the edge and then tied in a neat little bow under my chin. When I was escorted out the treatment room and through the doctor's waiting room, I wanted the floor to open up and swallow me whole. Dogs, cats, and I think there may have been a ferret or hamster waiting to be seen, all barked and stared at me. I could feel their gazes, gawks, and glares. I was horrified. To compound the entire scene, I thought something had happened suddenly to my eyesight. Since having that mechanically molded piece of petrochemical attached to my throat, my peripheral vision had virtually disappeared. I honestly thought I'd been drugged or poisoned. And so I was embarrassed, scared, and sure I was about to go to the big kennel in the sky. Fortunately, Bunny came to my rescue. When we arrived home, she removed the cone shaped gizmo and replaced it with something a bit less intrusive. I think she felt bad for me having to appear in public wearing something that resembled a medieval torture device.

Needless to say, the alternative wasn't perfect but it was far better than what the doctor had ordered. First, Bunny made me promise not to nibble, lick, taste, bite, or slobber the area where the growth had been removed. Then, wow – I'm not sure you're going to believe this – but she made me wear a life preserver. No really, and we were nowhere near any large bodies of water. Well, perhaps it wasn't an approved personal flotation device, but it sure looked like one. It was a soft piece of rubber tubing, covered in a velvet-like fabric, and then inflated with Bunny's own hot air. That was attached to my own collar (the one with the pendant) and placed around my neck. It wasn't great, but it was sure better than that cone-shaped gadget. She only insisted I wear it for a day, but that was already far too long for my taste.

You should know by now that being the queen *is* important to me, but I'm a compassionate ruler who cares deeply for her people. As I mentioned, our family extends far beyond the three of us. Most of the time it's just Bunny, Bud, and me in the house, but our clan includes many more canines and their people. Shortly after I joined the family, we went to visit the oldest member of their pack. I had no clue where we were going, but I was ready for a field trip. Bunny's father,

Herbert, lived a quick ten-minute ride from our house. It was the perfect distance and I spied a frozen yogurt shop and an Asian take-out bistro just down the street from his place. (I made a mental note of those establishments for future reference.) I later learned there was a wonderful park, duck pond, and walking path just behind Herbert's place. As we entered his building, I had a flashback to the apartment building where I was born. To be truthful, my anxiety level spiked just a bit as we walked into the lobby to wait for the elevator, but that soon subsided.

This was a very different place. Rather than being filled with young families and their dogs, this was a building filled with people who were much older than anyone else I'd ever met. Herbert lived alone and seemed genuinely pleased to see us. My guess is that he knew I was coming that day, because there was an unopened box of dog treats in his apartment, and he didn't even live with a dog. He scratched the top of my head and behind my ears, which is generally a sign that the person likes you. From that moment on, Herbert and I developed an understanding. I welcomed the treats and the scratches and while he wasn't ready to kiss me, he clearly appreciated my weekly visits.

I was also aware of Bunny and Bud's son, Elliott, as soon as I joined the family. Even though he was away at college when I selected them at the boutique, I felt his presence even before I met him face-to-face for the first time. Photos of him seemed to be everywhere, including a prominent portrait of him with Snowball. I could tell by his expression in the photo how much he must have loved her. Often times when I was home alone in the house, I liked to nap on Elliott's bed. I'm not certain if it was the soft comforter and pillows or the photos of that huge place at East 161st Street in The Bronx, but I was inexplicably drawn to his room. The first time we actually met, there was no question we were part of the same pack. We both loved our people, vanilla ice cream, steak, and taking walks around the neighborhood. Sure, he teased me once in a while, but I could dish it out as much as any other sibling. I knew it was all in good fun and there was never any malice or hard feelings.

Our first meeting was many years ago and now Elliott has his own family, including his wife Kathy, son Robby, and a loveable pooch. Sammy adopted them through a caring canine agency that specializes in matching older special-needs dogs with families. He'd been dumped in the Arizona desert before being arrested by the canine cops. I'd like to think that I played a part Elliott's conscious decision to ask a senior canine to adopt their pack. My ego may be just a bit inflated, but perhaps I served as a role model by providing unconditional love to the family, a quality that's now been passed down to another generation. Like me, Sammy's incredibly fortunate to have found a family who's eager to serve him.

Back when I was a much younger dog, Bunny and Bud used to leave the house to go to their places of employment. I recall there were occasions when Bunny was visibly distressed when returning home from work. I'm not sure why she was so troubled, but suffice it to say she needed a sympathetic paw to hold. Seeing her so upset always made me feel terribly sad. As the family's alpha female, I knew it was my responsibility to console and support her. Although she didn't want to discuss the specifics with me, Bunny knew I was there for her, and that gave us both great comfort. Never forget, to reassure and love your person may be one of the most important things you can do for them.

Beyond my immediate pack, there were others in my circle who always made me feel welcome. We weren't exactly related and they didn't live with us, but from my perspective, they were like an extended family. Their territory abutted our property and we became the best of friends. Chilly, Echo, and Blizzard were pooches who loved me like a long-lost sister. We'd run around the yard together, sniff each other, chase chipmunks, roll in the grass, and simply appreciate each other's companionship. They even taught me how to listen for moles burrowing under the grass. Knowing my canine contemporaries were nearby and I could meet-up with them on most days was very comforting. They understood me, gave me advice on acclimating into a new situation, and it was just nice to know there was someone I could talk to – and who cared.

You should now understand that you are part of a family and that your family is your pack. You're still an individual with unique thoughts and feelings, but don't forget that your actions will likely impact those around you. Be kind and compassionate. Listen to others and don't prejudge people until you've had an opportunity to get to know them.

Review the checklist on the following page to assess your canine emotional intelligence.

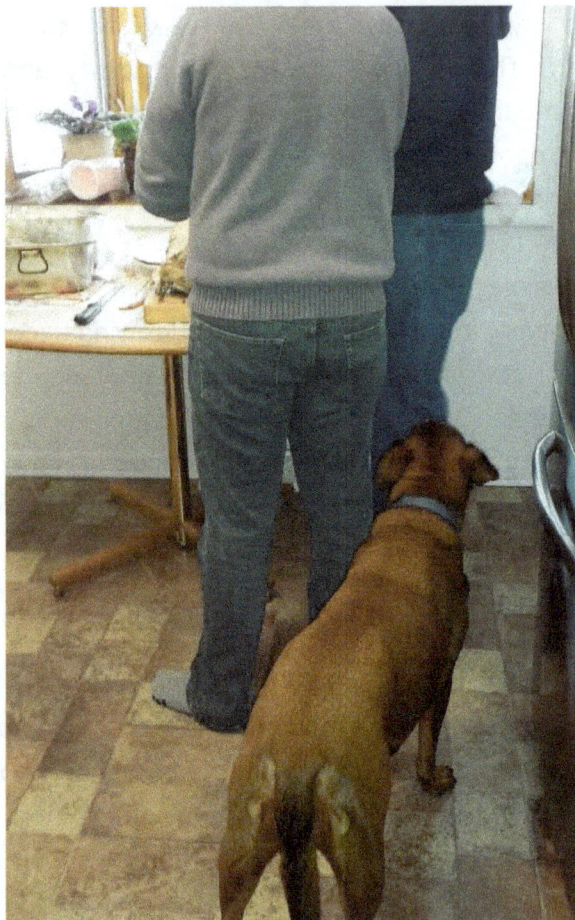

1. **Are you cognizant of your feelings and the feelings of those in your pack?**

Yes   _____

No   _____

Unsure   _____

If yes, your self-awareness and sensitivity to others make you a vital member of your pack. You've established yourself as the focal point of the household. I applaud your caring and compassionate sense of self.

If no, you may want to embark on a journey of self-assessment to learn who you want to be. A self-centered dog (or person) who only cares about themselves is too sad for words. Perhaps if you spent a night or two – or even three – in the clink, you'd have a different perspective on those who've devoted their life to you.

2. **Are you a good listener and a nonjudgmental friend to those in your pack?**

Yes   _____

No   _____

Unsure   _____

If yes, your pack is very lucky you adopted them. You may rise to be a ruler – sooner than later. You may want to consider volunteering as a mentor with other dogs.

If no, you may want to enroll in a personal relations communication course. You may also want to consider the deep-seeded reasons for your lack of compassion and ability to care for others.

3. <u>Do you realize or even care that your pack is willing to take the extra step for you?</u>

Yes   _____
No   _____
Unsure   _____

If yes, you are in touch with your feelings. You're cognizant of the fact that without your people, your life may have taken a very different – and perhaps sad and scary path.

If no, I recommend you take some time to volunteer at the local doggy detention center. Perhaps you've forgotten or have never even witnessed how those who're down on their luck spend every single day and night. If you're reading this book, you clearly have people who love and care for you.

4. Do you strive to think of ways to motivate your pack; to enhance their mood?

Yes   _____

No   _____

Unsure   _____

If yes, you've learned to communicate positive vibes through tail wagging and kisses. You are clearly in touch with your feelings, as well as the feelings of those around you. As a compassionate canine, you may want to consider a career as a counselor.

If no, you should realize your pack needs you and loves you. Show them you love them too. Don't waste your time sleeping, lounging, and languishing. You should strive to become a productive member of the pack.

Step Six: Bad Things May Happen to Good Dogs

✓ **At the end of Step Six, you'll understand the importance of unconditional love and how it can liberate you from awkward situations.**

> NOTE: The previous five steps focused primarily on how to adjust to life in your pack. You've learned how to communicate with your family, as well as care and educate them in a kind and compassionate manner. Although you may have had a rough start in life, for the most part – things have gone your way since rising through the ranks to become a monarch.

The intent of this lesson isn't to scare you. Then again, it's vital to be aware that incidents may occasionally happen in life which could have a direct effect on you and/or your pack. It's a doggone shame that more dogs aren't cognizant of this very fact. I'm not suggesting that you may be to blame for such occurrences, but it is possible that you may hypothetically and unintentionally have superficial roles in precipitating the genesis of these incidents.

As you read the following, you may get the impression that some of the situations described don't illustrate bad things happening to me at all. I can understand how one may be misled into thinking *I* was the catalyst for unfortunate things happening to others, but rest assured, that's simply not true. My rationale is quite straightforward. When my pack is excited, I'm excited; when they're hungry, I'm hungry; and when my pack is injured, I'm injured. It's really rather simple. As a kindhearted canine, I feel what my people are feeling. The following are unfortunate examples of such episodes.

I remember the day as if it were yesterday. Bud was at work, Scooter was home, and Bunny and I decided to go for a casual stroll around the neighborhood. It was a beautiful warm sunny day. Bunny's leash was attached to my collar, and she held the other end in her left paw. It was fall and the uncultivated wild animals – rabbits, squirrels, and chipmunks – that lived nearby were busy gathering provisions for the coming winter. The emotionally-aware part of my psyche honestly felt sorry for them. Having to scavenge, skimp, and save enough food for an entire season must be quite worrisome, as well as physically demanding. In fact, the very notion of going more than a week or two without a fresh supply of takeout from one the local Asian or Italian bistros is enough to spike my anxiety level.

Regrettably, sometimes the inner instincts buried deep down in my canine DNA take over, and even though there's no need for me to hunt or scrounge for my next meal, on rare occasions I feel an uncontrollable urge to hunt the little critters. Some may say what happened was solely *my* fault, although I beg to differ. Other than those directly involved in the incident, there were no first-hand fact witnesses and, I might add, there were no audio or video recordings of what transpired.

And so, a particularly large creature, I actually can't recall whether it was a colossal squirrel or an oversized chipmunk, ran across the road in front of us.

It reminded me of one of those prehistoric creatures I'd seen in documentary-style films. The gigantic rodent startled Bunny and I needed to defend her at all cost. As the alpha female – that was my job – my responsibility. I jerked Bunny's leash in an attempt to chase down the varmint, but then I heard a dreadful sound come from her mouth. It was a cross between a bark, a yelp, and a yowl.

For some unknown reason, Bunny failed to release her end of the leash and, instead, it jammed up underneath the rings she was wearing. Apparently as I surged forward to fight the malicious rascal, her leash twisted and then snapped the bone in her finger. I didn't actually hear it break, but I knew what had happened. Obviously, I felt terrible about the entire incident, but she remained remarkably composed. Sure, she was in pain, but Bunny kept telling me it wasn't my fault. Then again, her stoic behavior was really quite something to observe. If she'd asked, I would have finished our walk, but I made an executive decision that we should return home. I must say that I was so proud of how she handled the entire situation. On the other hand, I was a tad disappointed that our afternoon stroll was curtailed by this regrettable occurrence.

Well – long story short – she went to see her vet an hour later. When she returned home, I eavesdropped on her phone conversations with extended members of our pack, describing how the doctor had cut her rings off with a tool that resembled special shears. From what I understand, she was starting to lose circulation to her left front paw. It's terrifying to think that the actions of that ginormous animal had resulted in a spiral fracture of the proximal phalanx on Bunny's left ring finger. As someone with no medical training, I have absolutely no clue what that even means, but afterwards it was wrapped in an oversized bandage for the longest time.

For days following, I felt like a pariah within the pack. No one outwardly blamed me, but I did feel just a tiny bit guilty. I would never do anything to intentionally injure any of my people, but for some reason I felt as if I was to blame, even though that human-sized rabbit was obviously at fault. I just told myself that this too would pass and soon enough things would improve. Bunny held no apparent animosity toward me, but deep down it is conceivable she may have been just a bit perturbed. Perhaps if I hadn't felt the need to defend her against the mammoth-sized squirrel or chipmunk or rabbit or whatever it was, she wouldn't have been injured.

Perhaps my loyalty to her was just too much. Perhaps I was ready to go to battle to defend her honor at all costs, or perhaps I'm just deluding myself into pretending I had nothing to do with her injury. I wanted to hide, but I wanted to kiss her and apologize. I couldn't pretend nothing had happened, so I decided the most meaningful thing I could do was to simply sit quietly by her side and look at her with deeply mournful eyes. That's an important skill all dogs should master. It isn't really one of my specialties, but I had the presence of mind to implement that time-honored and reliable strategy. This sorry situation required I communicate my deepest regrets, even though she was as much to blame as I was.

Much later in life, Bunny and I had another unfortunate incident, which was clearly *not* my fault. As I mentioned in a previous lesson, I enjoy a good piece of steak as much as the next dog. And so, Bunny had read somewhere (probably in some cockamamy canine magazine) that bones are not good for dogs. I mean, really. Dogs and bones have a longer history than anyone can recall. It's akin to saying melted butter isn't good for lobsters or mice aren't good for cats. The entire premise is absolutely ridiculous, if you ask me. Needless to say, no one has asked me. To her credit, Bunny figured that perhaps I could enjoy devouring the meat off the bone, smell the bone, savor the bone, and lick the bone while never actually having the bone. Yes, she's just a tad indulgent, but we are the only two females in our immediate pack. It was a bit awkward at first, but I was ready to give it a go.

The day of the incident, Bud had grilled a beautiful piece of meat over charcoal. The aroma was beyond amazing and I figured it would be like any other meal. They would carefully slice bite-sized morsels of perfectly cooked steak and serve them to me on my plate.

After we all enjoyed our dinner, a new and unexpected step was added to our dining routine. Bunny took the plate with the bone and sat down on the floor next to me. She held the steak bone in each paw with outstretched arms toward me. I couldn't believe my eyes. I'd never seen such a gorgeous sight. My person was holding out an oversized meat encrusted bone specifically for *my* personal enjoyment. Talk about climbing to the top of the pyramid – wow!

I started gently, just nibbling each bit of meat between my beautiful canines. I licked the bone and tasted the meat. The entire experience almost sent me into a trance. For a brief moment, I thought that perhaps the seasoning in the meat contained some sort of mind-altering components. I must have become hypnotized by the bone, but I started taking bigger and bigger bites and then the bone unexpectedly dropped from Bunny's paws onto the plate. As she yelped, it was if someone slapped me out of my stupor. I'd bitten her and a bright colored liquid – not juice from the meat – but Bunny's blood was dripping on the floor. When I saw what had happened, I suddenly felt queasy, woozy, and dizzy.

Apparently, I had been drugged, because I would have never done such a thing without being impaired. As with the leash incident, I felt terrible and incredibly guilty even though it definitely wasn't my fault. I'm not certain what kind of seasonings were on that steak, but whatever it was sent me into an altered state. And since I didn't apply the seasonings or request the bone, I was not to blame for her unfortunate injury. It took quite a while for the bleeding to stop, but since I'd had all my shots, as had she, there was no need for either of us to seek professional medical attention.

Once again, I snuggled up to her and showed her my deep mournful eyes. Seeing her wound made me feel terrible, but she recovered soon enough. All these years later, we still engage in this bizarre routine with steak bones, but now I make every effort to remain sober and sane and not injure the paw that feeds me.

🐕 🐕 🐕 🐕 🐕

Aside from incidents that involve injuries to members of your pack, there may also be times when for some unknown reason, you find yourself in highly embarrassing situations. I'm including the following examples in my lesson of bad things happening to good dogs, simply because I was so incredibly humiliated by both incidents. Now I'm not going to equate Bunny's unfortunate physical injuries with my emotional humiliation, but the follow examples remain lodged in my thoughts. While her broken bone and cut skin have long since healed, the anxiety associated with the following instances are still firmly embedded in my very being.

Living in the northeast region of the country was both beautiful and horrifying. I loved the aroma of the freshly cut grass, the fragrant flowers, the raspberries growing behind my house (and eating the juicy fruit right off the bush), the sounds of the birds, but the foliage in the fall was really something. Rolling and playing in the leaves and pine needles was invigorating – and even as a mature queen, I found genuine joy in this annual ritual.

Over the course of the season, my people would rake and mulch thousands of leaves, place them in enormous paper sacks, and then dispose of them. I generally kept a watchful eye on their work, which often included strolling and rolling through the piles as they worked to pick them up.

On one occasion in the midst of this yearly chore, I had a rather unfortunate incident. Apparently, I'd made a solid deposit out amongst the leaves and no one bothered to pick it up for me. Its burnt umber and russet color blended in so perfectly with the leaves, much like a chameleon. It was really rather amazing. Anyway, I must have had a bit of a head cold because I failed to notice its pungent aroma. It wasn't until after I rolled in the leaves that were stuck to it like glue, that

I realized there seemed to be sour scent being emitted from the back of my neck and shoulders.

At one point, Bud took a brief break from raking and walked over to speak with me about something (I don't honestly recall the subject of that conversation). He touched my back and he instantly realized his hand was covered in my chestnut colored deposit. Clearly, their failure to clean up after me wasn't my fault, but I bore the brunt of their obvious oversite.

Bunny and Bud immediately returned their rakes to the garage and the three of us quickly proceeded upstairs to hit the shower. They insisted I walk directly into the bathroom and then closed the door behind us. I suppose they didn't want me to hop up on their bed and roll around. Unlike most dogs who either go to the barbershop or beauty parlor for a shampoo and shave, my people prefer to bathe me in the privacy of our own home. Bunny only purchases organically-sourced and tear-free products for my exclusive use. Since I have naturally short hair, there's no need for a trim, so their shampoos suit me fine. Of course, normally I don't have such stinky stuff strewn across my back.

After several repetitions of the shampoo-rinse cycle, I was finally released from the shower. To think that I'd rolled in my own doggy-doo was enough of a humiliation, but to then be subjected to an extended time under the shower nozzle was the icing on the cake. Again: I was a victim of circumstance, but their love for me and my love for them helped us all to forgive and forget the entire stinky incident.

🐕 🐕 🐕 🐕 🐕

When it gets cloudy and cold in the northeast it often snows, and where we lived it wasn't unusual to have accumulations exceeding one or even two feet. Now you know I'm a dog – and dogs wear fur coats year-round. This isn't a covert piece of intelligence. During the winter months, my coat becomes a bit heavier, bulkier, and warmer. Even my paws toughen up in the colder weather. I'm not a vet or an expert in teaching or explaining the details of canine physiology, but believe me – it's true. I suppose if a dog doesn't feel up to par, perhaps with kennel cough or a common cold, they don't fare well in cold weather, but generally our bodies adjust quite well.

The same is true for most all breeds and so when my extended pack Blizzard, Echo, and Chilly saw me standing in our snow-covered driveway wearing a black fleece parka with a charcoal grey lining and matching boots, I was beyond embarrassed. Bud was busy pushing our oversized snowblower and Bunny was scraping the driveway with the shovel and I stood there like an onyx statue.

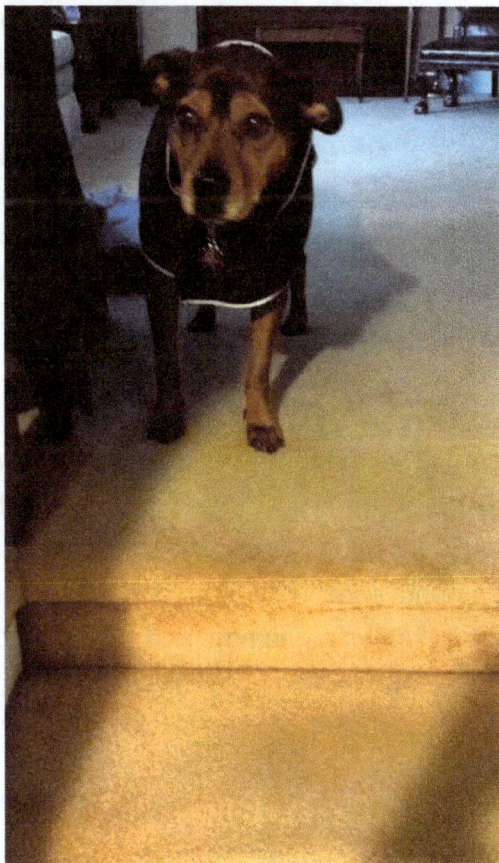

As I think back at being coerced into wearing that ridiculous outfit, I know Bunny and Bud's hearts were in the right place. They were simply concerned and perhaps a bit overly protective of me. That's a good thing – right? It's better to be loved too much, than not at all. I mean, I saw the label inside the coat's lining and it wasn't some piece of dreck from a third-hand schmata store. No, this was top quality material, finely sewn, with two zippered pockets for treats, but it just wasn't my style. I actually felt bad that they'd probably shelled out good money for this crazy get-up, but even so I admit I was more than a bit humiliated.

The parka's collar stood up around my neck and ears and there was a wide fleecy belt that went under my belly and attached on the side with Velcro. That was bad enough, but the boots were beyond ridiculous; four black fleece boots that attached with straps around each wrist and ankle. Between that binding belt under my tummy and the fact I couldn't really walk in those nonsensical boots; I was essentially paralyzed: frozen in place to the snowy pavement.

The three canines next door ran and jumped in the snow, and I stood there like some sort of catatonic cat. I could hear their laughs and see them staring at me.

They yelled at me to come over to play in the snow, but I couldn't move.

To make matters even more awkward, although the Velcro belt didn't obstruct my privates, I couldn't do my business while wearing that outlandish ensemble. Now I've *never* been known to have difficulties in that area, but I just couldn't go. I needed to go, but whether it was that belt around my tummy or simply a psychological inhibition at relieving myself while wearing what I knew was an expensive get-up, I honestly don't know.

After what seemed like an eternity, Bunny saw that I was terribly unhappy. I'm not certain why it took her so long to pick-up on my negative vibes, but suffice it to say she finally realized that playing dress-up with me was a big mistake. And so, I was both ecstatic and relieved when she finally set down her shovel and opened the door to the house, but not before insisting on taking a photo of me in that preposterous costume. A short time later, I told her I needed to go out, and as soon as she opened the door, I ran out into the driveway to relieve myself. That was the last time I ever wore the fleece parka with matching boots. I felt bad that the outfit had been such a fiasco, but not bad enough to wear it again. I'm only hoping that it was donated to a needy dog somewhere.

Review the checklist on the following page to evaluate how you would react to the four situations in this lesson. There are no right or wrong answers; however, I urge that you remain true to yourself.

1. **Imagine yourself walking your human – and the leash snaps their paw. Would you:**

Insist on finishing the walk   _____
Feel it was your fault   _____
Unsure   _____

Insisting on finishing the walk means you're an absolute ruler with no regard for your people.

If you feel you're at fault, that may actually be true. Be sympathetic to their pain and plight.

2. **While enjoying the meat from a bone, your canines injure your person's skin.**

They should be more careful   _____
OMG, I'm so sorry   _____
Unsure   _____

Thinking they should be careful is a valid response. Your person knew this could happen.

Feeling sorry for their injury indicates you are emotionally in-touch with your person. Bravo!

3. <u>You're supervising fall clean-up and you accidently roll in your own excrement.</u>

Your people should have cleaned up
your stinking mess   _____

It's your mess, deal with the
consequences   _____

Believing your people should clean up your
messes is absolutely on point. This is *their* job.

Believing it's your mess and you should deal with
the consequences is a defeatist attitude.

4. <u>Your person insists you wear a parka and boots, when you're already in a fur coat.</u>

They love you and only want to do what
they believe is right. Suck it up and wear
it   _____

Are you kidding me? I can't walk, I can't
pee, this is too humiliating for words   _____

Playing along with their dress-up game says
you're too submissive. Standup for yourself!

This humiliating must end – now! You know who
you are and you're not a dress-up doll

Step Seven: Personal Hygiene

✓ **At the end of Step Seven, you'll have a clear understanding of your pack's expectations surrounding personal hygiene routines and practices.**

NOTE: Personal hygiene is a touchy subject – one which many find intimidating to discuss in a public forum. If you're such an individual, I appreciate your anxiety – however I only ask that you contemplate why this topic makes you uncomfortable. My hope is that this lesson will lessen your embarrassment as you move forward in life.

Personal hygiene is an area many feel awkward discussing with others, let alone reading about in a guidance document. The very nature of the term implies that the subject matter is highly *personal.*

In researching this book, I considered whether or not to even tackle this incredibly sensitive topic and in truth, my typist and personal assistant Laura and I engaged in several lengthy conversations weighing the pros and cons of including this chapter. I know she's proficient at managing her cleanliness, as am I, although I admit on rare occasions, she and Bud do insist on offering me assistance. In truth, the simple fact that I lack opposing thumbs means I periodically welcome a bit of support: such as when my own dog doo from the backyard was inexplicably and unexpectedly pasted to the back of my neck. In the end, we both agreed that I owed it to my readers to address personal hygiene from my unique perspective. I've made every effort to present this material in a gender-neutral and unbiased manner.

Please take a moment to consider how *you* define personal hygiene. As a dog, I've observed that a human's interpretation of this very sensitive subject differs greatly from that of most canines. It's my understanding that the vast majority of people essentially believe personal hygiene addresses the overall cleanliness of their body for the purpose of ensuring good health. On the surface, this straightforward description sounds rather normal, but you may find the following protocols rather odd. I'm not certain I truly understand their unique method, but this is how I believe most people attempt to practice good personal hygiene. Regrettably, they have this narcissistic notion that their rules should be utilized by their entire pack – including their dogs.

Before starting their process, they commonly remove their clothing. Now I'm not so naïve to think there aren't dogs who also wear clothes (beyond their collars), but walking around in public wearing human-like clothes just isn't my thing. Sure, an occasional paisley bandana or kerchief to add a touch of flare to your appearance is one thing, but that's far different than donning an entire ensemble. Speaking for myself, I find jackets, coats, sweaters, and alike incredibly uncomfortable. As you learned in the previous lesson and to be perfectly frank, they impede my sense of movement, not to mention the fact they rub me in places I'd really rather not discuss.

And so, after removing whatever they're wearing, they step into a large vat of warm water or stand under a gizmo that mimics an intense rainstorm inside the house (more about that later). In addition to the water, they then apply some sort of perfumed cleaning concoction which they generally squeeze out of bottles. Sometimes the solution comes as a solid bar and is applied directly to their bare skin or onto a cloth, and then their skin. As it is mixed with the water, heavily scented bubbles form, which then need to be thoroughly doused with even more water until they disappear. I've encountered subtle floral-like scents, as well as those which are so strong, they make my eyes water.

When you think about this combination of behaviors, its actually fairly puzzling. I believe the intent of the exercise is to cleanse their body, but then to apply an odorous potion that results in something that wasn't there before and then needs to be removed with gallons of water, is a concept I simply don't follow.

To make it even more confusing, rather than smelling like a clean and natural person, they often reek like the aromatic and sometimes foul-smelling mixture they used when they were wet. While you may find this scent to be unpleasant, the person may truly believe it smells pleasant, as well as hygienic and sanitary. I've actually witnessed such acts and will address this later in this lesson. I'm only including this, because I don't want you to think humans have the ultimate answer to cleanliness. Clearly, they don't.

Before I go any further, I feel I must address a degrading and discriminatory myth about my fellow canines – both male and female. There are beings in the world who believe all dogs emit a certain pungent odor, which they find not to be entirely pleasant. I know you may be dismayed to see this in print, but it's absolutely true. Speaking as one who happens to savor the distinct and affable aroma of a dog, I find the suggestion that dogs often don't smell inviting to be absolutely offensive. To make such gross generalizations that dogs produce certain scents which most believe are unpleasant is, as I said, both degrading and discriminatory.

Clearly, not all dogs smell alike and I happened to savor the smell of certain types. For example: to think that French Poodles or Bulldogs and Russian Borzoi or Wolfhounds emit the same aromatic bouquet is ridiculous. The ones from France obviously smell like fresh baguettes and cheese, while the ones from Russia smell more like beet borscht and stroganoff (that's a dog joke).

Seriously, we all have our scents. I know people don't want to believe this, but even humans produce a unique scent. How else could a Bloodhound perform their job? This would be an ideal topic for a group discussion within your pack.

The real question is: why do humans, including mine, believe they're smarter than we are with regards to maintaining our own personal hygiene? Not only do they think they know more, they insist that our age-old methods, methods that have been handed down from generation-to-generation through both nature and nurture, are not effective, proper, or hygienic. Please try not to interpret the following examples in a negative or critical vein – nor think I am offering a professional medical opinion on this subject. I only offer these examples to illustrate my perspective as a canine, of how incredibly far many people go to impose their beliefs on their dogs. Also, I'm not claiming to be at all objective on this topic. It's just that I prefer managing my own hygiene.

Going back to my early days as a pup, I recall my mother teaching me about cleanliness. She'd use her long thick Pit Bull tongue to lick my tiny body from head to tail with her sweet-smelling saliva. They say that certain smells can make us recall distant memories and for me, the exquisite fragrance of Pit Bull sputum makes me think of my beautiful mother. Obviously, that's clearly my personal preference and you may prefer the smell of Beagle, Collie, or whatever your heritage encompasses.

My point is that, she cared for me enough to teach me about personal hygiene by doing what dogs have done for a dog's age: from the beginning of time. They use tongues as sponges and their drool as soap to clean themselves, friends, and families. Let me put this in simpler terms – dogs lick themselves. You know this. I know this. It's really that simple. Do we lick for enjoyment? Sure, but most of the time we lick strictly to clean our paws and the area immediately adjacent to our tails. I think people like to refer to this as grooming.

This brings me to my next point – or pet peeve. If we groom ourselves, why are we dragged, schlepped, and duped into going to a place known as a groomer? The answer is sad, but true. Even though most of us do a doggone good job at self-grooming, most people don't think our methods are effective. Now I know dogs who've been to those places known as dog washes, groomers, pet spas, and canine hairdressers and they're definitely not my cup of kibble.

First, they lure you through the door with something like a fresh peanut butter cookie or a piece of freeze-dried chicken breast. Everything's wonderful, for a moment, but then they douse you in a tub of water with some sort of stinky solution. They scrub your entire body, including between your toes. Sometimes they use a pair of sheers or other cutting implement to trim your hair or fur – in places I'd rather not mention. Your nails are trimmed, your ears are cleaned, and a gizmo is even used to brush your teeth. At the end they spritz an awful smelling perfume all over your frazzled and quivering body. In my humble opinion, the entire experience is a mental, physical, and sensory assault.

Yes: I know some dogs actually enjoy this process and I've heard that many people pay big bucks to pay for what I consider torture. My only response is that these dogs must be masochists. On the other paw, I also know some dogs, like people, do a lousy job of maintaining their own appearance, and for them a session with one of these beauty parlors may be a good thing. Of course, that's my own personal, non-medical professional, and highly subjective opinion.

Now I'm not saying a warm shower can't be enjoyable, perhaps once or twice per season, but the entire notion of enduring this process in the presence of total strangers must be absolutely terrifying and humiliating. As part of my training process with Bunny and Bud, I taught them to (1) save their hard-earned money for juicy treats rather than trips to the groomers and (2) that when I groom myself, I'm usually pretty darn effective. Okay there are times when I need a shower out of season, but those have been few and far between. As I mentioned or at least implied, under the right circumstances a warm shower can be a relaxing and pleasant experience. For me, this means showering with my pack. No: it's not what it sounds like. It's all done in a highly respectful and modest manner.

First, the water temperature is warm, but not hot; it's balmy, but not scorching; it's tepid, but not burning. Second, the goop, the soap, the solution, the concoction is all-natural and has a rather gentle and subtle aroma. It doesn't contain an overpowering perfume that makes you want to take another shower. Finally, a soft and supple cloth is used to massage my body with the cleanser. I hate to admit this and even though it's in print, don't quote me – but I actually find the entire shower process rather enjoyable.

Afterward, things turn a bit chaotic and I've trained Bunny to chase me like a rabbit. It's really quite funny watching her scurry around on the wet floor. She generally has at least three or four oversized towels on hand as she attempts to dry me before I shake the water off my body throughout the inside of the house. She's so incredibly predictable and I know every one of her moves – none of which work too well. After trying to corner me in the closet floor with the pile of towels, I almost always manage to evade her through a series of right-hand turns and zig-zags. It has taken years, but I've perfected my moves – all of which are based on offensive plays by football receivers.

Training my people to respect my approach to cleanliness was particularly important to me, and yet I know my story is relatively unique. Enabling me to shower in the comfort of my own home and on an "as-needed" basis has been wonderful. You may not be as fortunate as I am, but there's no need to give up hope. One day, your pack may suddenly wake up and behave as well as my Bunny and Bud. In the meantime, a combination of visualization, hypnosis, and deep breathing should be able to assist you in enduring regularly scheduled trips to the dog wash.

🐕 🐕 🐕 🐕 🐕

Speaking of personal hygiene, I need to tell you what happened to me during one particularly bad winter storm. As I've mentioned, the northeast part of the United States is known for having cold, snowy, and sometimes icy storms. Now you're probably wondering why I added this particular anecdote to the lesson on personal hygiene. As you're about to see, my rationale is really fairly straightforward.

And so, we had a terrible storm. If I recall correctly, it started as a heavy cold rain with lots of wind. As it got colder and colder, the rain turned to ice – not snow, not sleet, but ice. I trust you're following this description, but this may help you.

I did a bit of research and learned that freezing rain happens when water freezes on contact with a surface, creating a coating of ice on whatever the raindrops contact. Anyhow, as ice coats bushes and trees they become very heavy and brittle. This particular storm was so bad and the ice was so incredibly dense and heavy, huge branches snapped off of the tops of the trees in my backyard and we lost electricity at our house. Bud brought out the candles and the battery-powered radio, which was fine but as the hours went by, the house got colder and colder and colder until I could literally see my breath while standing in the kitchen. (As a side note, amazingly Bunny was able to locate a takeout place to buy us dinner. She navigated the icy roads to and from Jack's Asian Palace without incident and returned with a bag full of much needed sustenance. When she opened the containers containing the warm lo mein, moo shoo chicken, and rice, the fragrant wafts of steam filled the freezing cold room like billows of smoke being forced from a smoke stack. It was wonderful, but I digress – this note has absolutely nothing to do with personal hygiene.)

That night, there was no question that Bunny, Bud, and I were all going to cuddle together in their bed to stay warm. We all had full bellies and looked forward to snuggling under the countless comforters, quilts, and throws. I scrunched down under the covers over which they'd added many additional blankets, until I was litterly in-between their sock-covered paws. Okay: here's the part about personal hygiene. There I was underneath a top sheet and at least ten heavy blankets sandwiched between four stinky paws. I mean really! Sure, there was no hot water for showers, but it was all I could do to keep from becoming asphyxiated.

I must have started to gag because Bud held up the load of blankets with his knees and tried to wave fresh air inside my blanket encrusted cocoon with his hands. Eventually we all fell asleep, but the lesson is really quite simple. First, they could have taken a hint from me and licked their paws clean – much like I learned from my mother, and I do for myself on a routine basis. Second, people should make a conscious effort to maintain a fresh smelling body at all times and under all circumstances. You never know when you'll end up sleeping with your entire pack and you don't want anyone to suffocate.

Review the checklist on the following page to evaluate your innermost beliefs surrounding personal hygiene. As with some of the early self-evaluation exercises, there are no right or wrong answers; however I urge that you remain true to yourself.

1. **The natural fragrance secreted by most canines is exciting, alluring, and stimulating.**

Yes   _____

No   _____

Unsure   _____

If yes, you are a dog who understands the critical importance scent has played for all canines since the beginning of time. You appreciate your heritage, your genetic makeup and believe preserving this age-old method of communication is essential to our genus.

If no, you've either lost your sense of smell or you've been brainwashed into thinking there is something unpleasant or putrid about our natural odor. If your nose is on the fritz, I recommend a visit to your doctor's office. If you believe our natural aroma is nasty, perhaps if you follow the lessons in this book, you'll be able to regain your self-confidence as a dog.

2. <u>You take pride in maintaining your own personal hygiene.</u>

Yes   _____
No   _____
Unsure   _____

If yes, you have a strong sense of self, you're comfortable in your own fur, and your confidence is contagious. Keeping yourself clean is a testament to your canine dignity and pride. Bravo, my friend.

If no, I'll only assume you enjoy being trimmed, shampooed, conditioned, and dried at the salon. I'm well aware of the fact that many dogs, as well as people, find this process relaxing and enjoyable. There's nothing wrong with bathing naked in a public place, it's just not my cup of kibble.

3. Do you believe dogs can maintain their cleanliness without the assistance of people?

Yes   _____

No   _____

Unsure   _____

If yes, you recognize the potency of dog drool to clean most any mess. Perhaps it's drool's natural chemical balance that makes it so effective, but I agree that a hearty application of canine saliva does wonders on most messes. There are rare occasions that require outside intervention, but again: those situations are the exception and not the rule.

If no, perhaps you need to increase your intake of liquids. Perhaps you're simply not producing adequate drool to do a decent job. Or you may have been persuaded by your people that you're helpless and can't manage your own affairs. Be bold – think for yourself.

Step Eight: Vacationing away from your pack

✓ **At the end of Step Eight, you'll learn that your people may, on occasion, send you on all expense-paid vacation. This isn't the worst thing in the world, provided you stay in at least a three-star resort.**

NOTE: You're clearly a vital part of the pack. Your family dotes on you and look to you for guidance and encouragement. No family, no pack is without its occasional disagreements and conflict and spending every day with each other can be nerve-wracking. Watching over your pack can be exhausting, so spending time away from each other provides an opportunity to focus on your own needs for a while. Take advantage of the vacation, this time away from your people.

If you're secure with your pack, your people, your family, you should welcome a bit of time away from each other. Don't worry that you're getting dumped, or what some who try to be politically correct refer to as being "rehomed". That newly invented term, rehoming, is just a fancy way of saying you're no longer welcome. Obviously, things happen. People get sick or they don't have the financial wherewithal to care for you, but to use the title rehoming is an insult. They owe it to you to be honest about the pack's situation. If you're unfortunate enough to learn you're about to be rehomed, I'm sorry – but you may want to skip this chapter. This lesson is designed for those dogs who rule the roost and are simply being sent away for a vacation, a spiritual retreat, or some time at the spa.

I remember the first time I was sent on vacation. I watched as my people packed suitcases with their clothes, bathing suits, toiletries, and assorted items. Everything seemed copacetic, especially since my things were also packed into my own overnight bag. My pillows, blankets, food, and even my memory foam bed was loaded into the back seat of our car. When we all piled in for what I assumed would be a glorious adventure together, I was overjoyed at the thought of us all hitting the road. Regrettably, I thought it was odd when Bud pulled into a driveway and started unloading the car after only about ten minutes on the road. I'm not naïve, and when I saw that it was only my luggage being unloaded and not theirs, I got very nervous. It was terrifying to think that I was getting the old dumperoosky: being sent back to the clink. I mean – really – what else could be happening? On the other paw, it didn't resemble a jail, not even a half-way house. I spied a few dogs running around in an oversized grassy backyard and they all looked fairly content. Still, I'm not ashamed to admit that the situation was somewhat unsettling.

My family kissed me goodbye, told me to be a good girl (how humiliating), and they'd be back to pick me up. That was it. They drove away and there I was in the home of a complete stranger with strange dogs, but as you know I'm what some would refer to as a tough gal. I'm a survivor, as flexible as a rubber bone, as sturdy as fire hydrant, and as secure as a leash on a collar. The woman in charge of the establishment gathered my things and asked me to follow her to my room. Okay: it wasn't exactly a room. In truth it was a big open kennel in her finished basement, but that was fine. It was actually quite cozy and since I had my own bed and linens it was really rather nice. On the other paw, there was no turn down service and the staff didn't fold towels to resemble rabbits or birds.

After getting settled, I was introduced to the other guests who were also staying in her place. If I recall correctly, we played some simple games to break the ice and to gain a sense of trust for each other. I told them my life story about being incarcerated in The Bronx and so on and so forth. I learned that a couple of my fellow lodgers had also been in the lock-up for minor infractions. It was sort of like taking part in a group therapy session. Instead of worrying so much about my people, this was my time to simply care for my own emotional and physical wellbeing. It was time to commiserate with others who'd led similar lives. Instead of feeling like I was excluded from my pack's trip to wherever they were going, this was my time to refocus my spirit, my soul, on what's most important in life: me.

One night, we all lay on our backs out in the yard and gazed at the stars together. I don't recall ever having been so incredibly relaxed and at ease with myself. One of the other dogs that was there that night, I think his name was Sirius, told us a story that long before anyone we know was born, people named stars and then made up pictures in the sky by tracing the stars with their paws. He told us about the best and brightest star – a star named Alpha Canis Majoris or the Dog Star – and also known as Sirius. He even pointed it out to us. It was such a revelation to learn that our storyteller was named for that star, I actually became overcome with emotion and started howling to the night sky. That behavior was entirely out of character for me, but that instinctual sound just seemed to flow out of my furry muzzle. It was almost as if my body was set on autopilot and some sort of ancient urge took over my entire being. Beyond the physical part of howling to the sky, it was such an emotional release for me. I don't think I'll ever forget Sirius or that night together.

We were all sad to see him go when he got picked up by his people a couple of days later. The place just didn't seem the same without his insight into the night sky. After I got home from what I referred to as my retreat, I tried to tell my canine pack pals, Echo, Chilly, and Blizzard about Sirius, but they didn't believe a word of my story. They just figured the entire story was an old dog's tale, but I personally believed every word of it. Regrettably, the woman who owned the place and allowed dogs to spend their vacations with her moved away and I never crossed paths with Sirius again. Be that as it may, he'll always have a special place in my heart and in my soul.

🐾 🐾 🐾 🐾 🐾

The following year, I think it was during a period that people refer to as the dog days of summer, once again it was time for vacation. Since I clearly couldn't return to my previous location, Bunny, Bud, and I went in search of an alternate place for my annual retreat. We wanted to tour a few sites to be sure they were up to my standards – and theirs.

The first place we saw was like a scene out of a horror film. It was so bad, I started looking around for that odd-looking boy with the banjo on the porch. As soon as we got out of the car, we could hear dogs sobbing and yapping in some sort of old dilapidated barn. I spied a malicious looking cat lurking around the outside of the place, making hissing sounds at the dogs locked-up inside. When the feline saw Bud and me, it turned and sprayed some sort of liquid from its backside, and then scurried over to the other side of the yard. It was both incredibly rude and uncivilized.

I felt as if we'd been transported into a place where dogs are summarily tortured – or worse. We took a quick look around and then high tailed it back to the car. We couldn't get out of there fast enough. Just being on the premises was enough to make me shed a load of fur, which I generally only do in the summer or if I'm exceedingly nervous. If I recall correctly, I think

I even tossed my biscuits near our car at the stress of being in such a place. That brief encounter was many years ago, and yet I still – on occasion have nightmares where I've been forced to go inside that barn.

I was incredibly upset by our five-minute visit to that horror show of a place, and Bunny and Bud felt so guilty at having even considered that place for me, that they immediately took me out for a barbequed chicken and rib dinner in Saratoga Springs. They understood my stomach was simply upset from the stress and not from being ill. It was actually a win-win excursion. The delicious dinner absolved them of their wrong-doing and I devoured every last bit of poultry and pork.

🐕 🐕 🐕 🐕 🐕

We clearly needed to continue our search for an appropriate place. So, a few days later we drove to a lovely location in the country which would have been fine, but it was a bit of a schlepp from our house to reach the new lodging option. We drove far out into the country until we reached a large house up on a hill. My initial thought was staying in that house would be great, but then the man that lived there took us on an extended walking tour of the property.

The dogs that lodged at his place didn't stay with him; instead, each dog vacationed in their own cabin set along the edge of a beautiful lake. It was truly amazing. Each bungalow had two rooms (a complete kitchen and bedroom), a TV and VCR (this was years before CDs and Blu-Rays), and a screened-in front porch that overlooked the water. There were a couple of Labs swimming in the lake, while a Terrier and a Corgi were working on their tans nearby. Cool bowls of water, biscuits, and raw-hide chews were even set out on beach towels along the water's edge for the guests. I was ready to sign up for a stay right then and there, but since it had taken close to an hour to reach the resort, I was overruled and we kept looking for the perfect place for me.

On our third attempt, we finally found nirvana. It didn't look like much from the outside, but there was a big picture of a smiling pink Poodle on the side of the building. Some dogs would have found that site rather unsettling, but I thought it looked like a place where dogs are probably pampered. Wow, I was right on target. Each dog had their own suite, with cable TV, chairs, air conditioning, and a bed. Plus (are you ready for this), each room was decorated in a unique style with an explicit geographic theme. There was a room that looked like a luxurious villa in the tropics, one that resembled a mountain top lodge; well you get the idea. The place also had a spa, complete with grooming and massages. You know how I feel about grooming, although the notion of a full body massage and professional pedicure definitely piqued my interest.

Bunny and Bud were equally impressed and that's where I spent several vacations and long weekends until we moved away from New York (more about that in the following lesson). It wasn't as homey as the place where I met Sirius, but it was far better than most places where people send their dogs for a vacation getaway. Review the following checklist to evaluate how you would react to the lodging options described in this lesson. As with the previous self-assessment, there are no right or wrong answers, but remain true to yourself.

1. <u>Imagine yourself being sent on vacation without your pack. Is this welcome or not?</u>

Yes   _____

No   _____

Unsure   _____

If you answered yes, I agree that a little separation once in a while is a good thing. It makes reuniting that much sweeter – plus it's good to get out and meet new dogs.

If you answered no, I also agree with this response. I know what it's like to be homesick, not to mention the fact that you generally need to eat of dog food while away. No steak. No chicken. No way.

2. <u>You don't really care where you vacation.</u>

Yes   _____

No   _____

Unsure   _____

If you answered yes, you really need to assess your standards of care. Dogs, like people, deserve to be well cared for: don't settle for the bare minimum. Strive for excellence.

If you answered no, I admire your doggedness and tenacity in a desire for mints on your pillow and a towel warmer in the bathroom.

3. <u>Choose between a rustic cabin at the lake or a posh bed and breakfast:</u>

Cabin	_____
B & B	_____
Unsure	_____

If you opted for a rustic cabin, first be certain there are no spiders or field mice. Rustic doesn't mean dirty, but it doesn't mean luxurious either. It could be fun to quasi-camp in the country.

If you opted for the bed and breakfast, there's an excellent chance the linens will be soft and fluffy – as will the eggs (cooked to order) at breakfast.

Step Nine: Caring for your Pack

✓ **At the end of Step Nine, you'll understand the importance of caring for your family. As a monarch, you have a moral obligation to ensure everyone in your pack is happy and the household runs smoothly.**

NOTE: Being a ruler is serious business, with a great deal of responsibility. You need to keep everyone on track, boost morale, and act in the best interest of the pack as a whole. Don't be selfish. Narcissistic dogs (and people) with big egos may think no one notices or cares about their self-absorbed behavior, but this couldn't be further from the truth. As the leader, they look to you for love, support, and guidance. Don't let them down.

Very few dogs are automatically chosen lead to their families. Most of us work our way up the ladder. Some, like me, start life in the sub-basement – below the lowest rung of the ladder of life. Others may start as apprentices, transition through middle-management, and eventually emerge as leaders in their pack. Regardless of how you came to be in your family hierarchy, it's my belief that those of us who enter life as unwanted pups and are fortunate enough to overcome our humble beginnings, often make the most empathetic and sympathetic leaders.

Please don't think that a compassionate leader is a pushover or a sucker. Speaking for myself, I always strive to act in ways to enhance and enrich the entire pack. I'm well aware of the fact that Bunny and Bud require continual guidance, in addition to compassionate care. This includes a wide range of issues which include ensuring they engage in adequate physical exercise, as well as reminders not to forget to take me on periodic shopping excursions.

Physical workouts can encompass a large variety of activities. You may find this strange, but many people pay significant sums of money to go to spartan warehouse-like structures with music blaring through loud speakers specifically to grunt, groan, and excrete a bodily fluid called sweat from their foreheads and armpits. These places are called gyms and needless to say, the pungent aroma of large groups of sweating people all in one place can be overwhelming. Why they spend good money to sweat – money that could otherwise be used to buy a roast turkey dinner – remains a mystery.

I care for my people by ensuring they stay far away from such places by exercising with them on long walks through the park. My job is to keep the pace: not as slow as a Basset Hound, but not as brisk as a Greyhound either. Our walks provide us all with much needed physical exercise. Like most dogs I thoroughly enjoy laying on the couch and watching a nature show or dog agility competition. On the other hand, the intellectual part of my brain tells me to get my tail in gear and start moving. And so, our pack takes daily walks together. It saves them money and exercising as a family provides an opportunity for us all to bond, enjoy nature, discuss current events, and then stop for fat-free frozen yogurt afterwards. (In truth, I prefer ice cream, but frozen yogurt is a healthier option and isn't too bad if you cover it up with hot caramel, butterscotch, chopped walnuts, and gobs of whipped cream.)

There are a few points to remember when leading your pack on these walks. First, be certain your person carries at least two or three disposable bags for picking up any deposits (aka dog doo) you may dump while on the trail. This is just good walking etiquette. I've seen many others fail to pick up their dog's deposits, and I can't tell you how embarrassing it is to witness such disgraceful behavior. If I thought someone was at risk of putting their paw in something that came out of my backside, I would be doggone horrified. Just writing this guidance is embarrassing, and yet unfortunately it's also necessary.

The second point to remember is to keep up a good pace while walking. Now you're not out to break any land speed records, but you're not a slug or a sloth either. Walking at a decent clip will provide everyone with a respectable workout. Your people need to walk, and not just stroll. On the other hand, they don't need to trot or jog or even do-si-do, but they should walk at least fast enough to keep up the pace you set for them. Ideally, they should get their heart-rate up just a bit, but not to the point where emergency responders are summoned to revive them.

If there's another pack walking in front of you, be polite and don't put your nose up the tush of other dogs. Your instincts may tell you to move in for a deep dive. In truth, there's nothing quite like the sweet-smelling aroma of a Pug or a Bulldog, although you need to exercise self-control, as well as your muscles. Yes, I enjoy inhaling the fragrance of another dog's privates as much as the next dog, but there's a time and a place for everything. A walk with your pack is neither that time or that place. If it seems you're getting too close to a dog walking ahead of you, either slow the pace or check your mirrors, signal, and then pass them on the left.

The third point is that you may encounter unusual objects when out for a walk. Exercise extreme caution when sniffing unidentified decomposing organisms along your route. Your person may think an item is perfectly harmless, when in reality it may actually be a discarded piece of rubbish – or worse yet, the remains of a deceased rodent. Just stay on the path, keep your eyes forward, and don't look for trouble. I remember on more than one occasion when my nose was only millimeters away from a physical encounter with a poisonous mushroom. Exploring off-trail simply isn't worth the bother. Remain focused on exercising your person, and all should be fine. This will keep them happy and you out of trouble.

I would be derelict if I didn't share another activity other than walks that your pack can, and should engage in to get much needed exercise. Early on in our relationship I made it quite clear that although we resided in a climate where frozen precipitation was the norm in the winter, there was no reason whatsoever that I should squat naked in a snowbank to relieve myself. The very notion that a delicate dog such as me should be coerced, coaxed, or cajoled into such a humiliating act was absolutely abhorrent. Be strong and communicate like I did.

If your people open the door with the expectation that you're going to (1) enjoy stepping into a snowbank or (2) be enticed into peeing in a pile of frozen ice crystals that's so high it encompasses your entire tail or (3) not care that your tush is flash frozen as soon as you squat – listen to me carefully. Don't do it. Stand your ground. Don't move, shuffle, or even slide your paws off the warmth of the carpet into a snowbank. Run and hide somewhere in the depths of your house. They'll get the message. You may think this is an act of belligerence, but in fact it's actually demonstrating how much you love and trust your people. They know you only have their best interest at heart.

In our family, it somehow became Bunny's task to employ the use of a large and sturdy shovel to clear a path for me to do my business. Be vigilant and supervise your person, but keep a safe distance. You don't want to give the false impression that a pristine path isn't truly necessary. Not only will this ensure the path meets your exact specifications with regards to its length, width, and depth, but by doing so it will have the added benefit of providing your person with much needed physical activity. I must say that over the years, Bunny became quite proficient at creating areas that even exceeded my exacting expectations. For example, if she shoveled an area and it kept snowing, or a strong gust blew snow back over what she had already cleared, she'd go back out and clean it up for me.

🐕 🐕 🐕 🐕 🐕

Shopping with your pack is the perfect time to show them how much you care for them. Depending on where you live, as well as the type of store, dogs may or may not be permitted. Yes: I know canines officially classified as service dogs, are always permitted. Please don't get me started on that point. The only thing I'll say is that I provide services to my people every day: my companionship, guidance, unconditional love, and overall supervision.

And so, even though I am not an authorized, certified, licensed, or sanctioned service dog, I am permitted to accompany my people into certain retailers. First and foremost, unlike the little test I gave them when we first met, be certain to do your business before entering the store. This will send a clear signal to your person how much you care about them. Obviously, accidents happen, but try not to embarrass yourself or your people. It's not a good look for anyone.

When taking your people shopping, take your time. Unlike an exercise walk, this *is* the time to stroll. If they wanted to run in and out for a single item, they wouldn't have brought you with them. When shopping, my people particularly appreciate the care I take in touring every aisle in the store. This is the perfect opportunity to savor the smells, touch the merchandise, and socialize with the other patrons. I recommend thinking of a store as one of those experiential museums where people can handle the exhibits. I particularly appreciate stopping to inhale the incredible scents emanating from the oversized sacks of dry food, strategically located at my nose and eye level. The various flavors and packaging are in fact, designed to attract the four-legged customers and their people.

It's peculiar, but when we're shopping together and my people see others who aren't accompanied by a dog, they're totally oblivious to them and just keep walking. In contrast, when they see someone who's shopping with a dog, they generally seem to stop and chat. As their mentor, I always nurture this type of social interaction. It provides them time to network with other like-minded people and having observed numerous encounters, I can tell you without hesitation that they genuinely appreciate such opportunities.

On a social-emotional level, conversing with those who shop with their dogs encourages your people to develop positive relationships with others. Obviously, it also gives me an opportunity to chat with the other dog as well and exchange tales. On the other hand, when complete strangers start petting my head and/or other regions of my body, it can be a bit awkward. When you think about it, invading my personal space and touching me without being granted permission is really rather presumptuous. If I decided to lick or even sniff a strange person's privates – well you can just imagine the reaction that would generate.

Even so, it's the doggondest thing, but perhaps dogs bond people to each other in a way nothing else can. I know there are those who are devoted to their cats, hamsters, and goldfish, but canine people are unique amongst mammals. You don't see people shopping with their felines or rodents. Even when they're not shopping, it's not unusual to see dogs in public places with their people. Dog-people may have nothing else in common, but they are obviously all devoted to their dogs. Their political and religious beliefs may be as disparate as preferring either sweet or salty snacks or even living as a vegan or an omnivore, but loving their canine companion erases the differences and brings them together. The more I think about it, maybe we are the key to resolving divisiveness amongst people and their packs.

Review the checklist on the following page to consider how you care for your pack.

1. __Exercising with your person is:__

A pain in the tail _____

A wonderful time to bond _____

Unsure _____

If exercising is a pain in the tail, you need to get over it and start moving. Life is too short.

If you think of exercising as the perfect time to bond, you're confident and caring.

2. __You don't care whether or not your pack clears an area for you when it snows.__

Yes _____

No _____

Unsure _____

If yes, you must be part Husky or very tall. Trust me, squatting in the snow is no day at the beach.

If no, you should make it quite clear that your delicate privates aren't designed to be flash frozen – and doing so could result in long-term health consequences.

3. <u>I believe caring for my pack is both an emotional and physical responsibility.</u>

Absolutely   _____

No way   _____

Unsure   _____

If you responded in the affirmative, I applaud you for your sense of worth in the pack.

In responding "no way", you're obviously egotistical and narcissistic. You need therapy.

4. <u>After going for a walk, you prefer fat-free frozen yogurt or ice cream:</u>

Fat-free frozen yogurt   _____

Ice Cream   _____

Unsure   _____

This is a trick question. Regardless of your response, you're my kind of dog.

5. <u>Shopping with your person is a chore.</u>

Yes   _____

No   _____

Unsure   _____

If yes, you should get out more and experience life. Sniff the bags of food and have fun.

If no, you know that shopping is a time to bond with your person and social with others.

Step Ten: Retirement and Moving West

✓ **At the end of Step Ten, you'll have gained insight into your pack's retirement and how that will impact you and your lifestyle.**

NOTE: People, as well as dogs, sometimes opt to move to a different geographic region when they retire from their places of employment. This is much different than a vacation. Relocating in retirement is akin to a fresh start; however, the core members of your pack move as a cohesive unit to a new home – often in a location you've never visited. This can be both unsettling, as well as exciting. I know not all people relocate to another place when they leave their places of employment, but mine did. If yours didn't, bravo for you, but this is my story and these are my lessons.

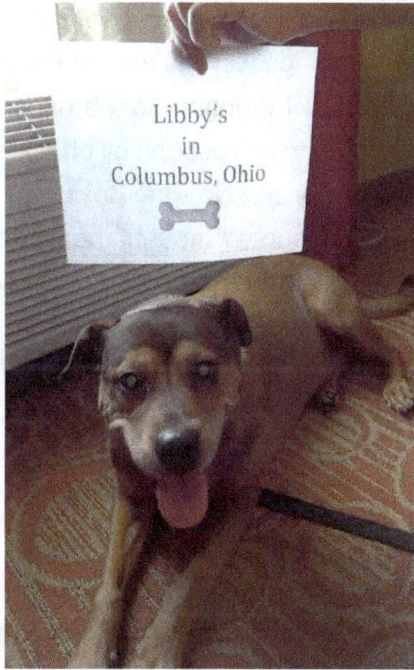

Libby's
in
Columbus, Ohio

I knew something unusual was going on when my pack decided to sell our house. People I only knew peripherally stopped by to visit and left with the oddest assortment of souvenirs – everything from large pieces of furniture to boots and jackets to Bud's giant snowblower. I assumed it was all on the up-and-up when I saw our things being loaded into other people's cars or carried into our neighbor's houses, but I really didn't know what was happening. It was obvious that we weren't being robbed, because Bunny and Bud watched as our things were taken out the door. To be completely honest, I thought that perhaps my people had hit the skids and needed to sell off our stuff to buy me kibble and steak. No one told me what was happening, so of course I thought the worst.

One day, a giant metal receptacle was delivered to our house and strategically positioned in the driveway. The empty container was filthy and emitted an unusually pungent odor. Suddenly things I'd never seen before were emerging from the darkest corners of the basement for the sole purpose of being unceremoniously dumped into the container. I sat and watched as Bud and Bunny tossed a wide range of things into the box. It was then that I realized this was no ordinary container, it was a dumpster reserved for disposing of unwanted belongings. Witnessing the removal of so many things from our house was very perplexing and worrisome. To be honest, the house was in such disarray it took all of my energy to keep track of my things. I was doggone worried.

Hundreds of books were packed into boxes; a wide assortment of winter coats, boots, and other clothes were stuffed into giant bags. Everything was placed in Bunny's car, and I never saw them again. I think she donated things to dogs and their people who were in need of cold weather gear, as well as fresh reading material – or something like that. With everything strewn about, it looked like a colossal boondoggle.

My number one fear was that some of my belongings were going to be given away or disposed of in error. An even bigger fear was that I was going to be given away or disposed of in error: no, really. I started having nightmares and flashbacks to my days in the streets of The Bronx. Perhaps it was that metal dumpster, but my anxiety level was not in a good place. It was disconcerting that not only was I not consulted about the move, but I wasn't even informed. It just happened. Believe me, I sincerely thought my relationship with Bunny and Bud was much stronger than that.

To this day, it's a mystery as to how or why we never engaged in a quiet rational conversation to address the intricacies and details of the relocation plan. I don't ask for much, but even if they'd provided me with a brief memo, a text, or an email outlining the strategy, the rationale for moving, and providing me with a day-to-day schedule, it would have gone a long way to ease my nerves. Perhaps the details were only divulged on a "need to know" basis and I was out of that loop or didn't have high enough clearance for this. By recounting those days in this guidance, many unsettled memories have rematerialized in my mind. When you learn what happened to my life, you'll understand my angst.

One morning I woke up as usual and the next thing I knew, all of my belongings were loaded into the backseat of Bud's car. I watched as the kitchen cupboards were systematically emptied. All my food – the dry, the wet, the treats, as well as my dishes, placemats, tablecloths – everything was packed into boxes and bags. They even packed up my beds, blankets, pillows, and the queen-sized quilt where I liked to lounge during the evening. I figured this is it: I'm getting the old dumperoosky. They're going to slap a *return to sender* sticker on my tush and I'll need to do my best to start a new life – again. What was I to think?

The next thing I knew, I was standing in the driveway by Bud's car. The car door was open and I could clearly see that the backseat was filled with all my things. My baggage and boxes were on the floor and my quilt were spread out on the seat. Between my beds, blankets, and bolsters, there was barely enough room for me to lay on the seat. Before we even went anywhere, I spied Bunny by her car. It was literally filled to the brim with cartons, clothing, and containers. The entire situation was very odd. I still had no clue what was happening. That's when it finally hit me.

🐕 🐕 🐕 🐕 🐕

My canine companions Chilly, Blizzard, and Echo came over with their person to wish us a safe journey. We all sniffed each other, and it seemed they knew more about what was happening than I did. Apparently, we were on the brink of a great one-way road trip. In other words, Bunny and Bud had no plans for us to return home – ever. Now I'd been on lots of road trips in the past, but we always came back to our house. Even when we traveled to places in Massachusetts and Vermont, we somehow managed to return. I still didn't know why we were going or where we were going, but I knew we were going, it was forever, and it was time to get in the car.

The first leg of our journey was, for the most part, uneventful. I managed to rearrange my pillows and blankets in the back of Bud's car, which made the trip fairly comfortable. As long as I was with my man, I figured things would probably be okay. I'd lost my fear of abandonment, although I still had no clue where we were headed. He and Bunny spoke to each other over radios, which was fairly odd. I kept hearing her voice, but she wasn't with us. Whenever I heard her, I checked the front seat, but all I saw was a pile of CDs, crackers, dog biscuits, bottles of water, and diet cola. It took me a while to realize she was in her car – just ahead of us. Usually our car trips don't last more than an hour, so once I'd been in the back seat for multiple hours, I was ready to get out and stretch my legs. After a quick potty break near a tree and a snack, we were back in our respective vehicles and that's when I decided that perhaps if I took a nap, I'd wake up from this doggone nightmare. Seriously: I enjoy a trip in the car as much as any other dog, but this was getting ridiculous. Obviously, we weren't going to the park or my favorite chicken and rib joint, since we could have made countless round-trips from our house and back again already.

After what seemed like a gazillion hours in the backseat and a few more potty breaks, we finally reached our destination. I knew we weren't in New York State anymore, because I'd noticed the road signs as we passed through Pennsylvania and into Ohio. You may be questioning my canine skills at reading, but since I'm dictating this book, obviously I'm really quite literate. Anyway, I think we were in a place called Columbus.

We pulled into a place that welcomed travelers who needed a comfortable place to sleep. I'd never stayed in a hotel: or even a motel, an inn, or a bed and breakfast, so this was going to be a first for me. Sure, I'd vacationed at the doggy spa, but that place was exclusively for dogs. Two legged guests simply weren't allowed. Therefore, the notion at staying overnight in a place with Bunny and Bud – other than home was all very exciting. The lobby of the building was decorated with pictures that resembled acorns or buck's eyes. I'm not certain I understood the significance of such an unusual theme, but it seemed pleasant enough. Bunny and Bud unloaded some things from our cars, including my bedding and we all moved into one-bedroom place together. It was beautiful – cozy, but not small – roomy, but not overwhelming, although I couldn't seem to locate the rest of the place. Unlike our house, everything seemed to be in one big space with a bed and TV, except of course there was a toilet, sink, and shower. I wasn't sure whether this was the end of the line or if this was just a stopover on our way to an unknown destination. As you should know by now, I'm amazingly adaptable – and since I wasn't paying the bill, I was willing to give this new place a go.

Well, we rested for a short while and then walked to a great burger restaurant for dinner. It was fantastic. I'd never heard of living in a place where you could simply walk across a parking lot to get to such an establishment. The tables outside the main restaurant were comfy, and they welcomed four-legged patrons. I decided right then and there, I could get used to living there. That night, we all slept together in one giant bed – Bunny, Bud, and me. There was no doubt I'd be very happy living in this new place.

That night while we rested, I thought I overheard a Mastiff, a Pug, and their family moving into the room next door to ours. I was anxious to meet them in dog – or person (depending on your unique perspective) and I made a mental note to stop by for a visit the next day. And so, after a delicious breakfast in the lobby of the place, I was ready to explore our new neighborhood and track down our neighbors. I was just about ready to embark on a cursory investigation when Bunny and Bud started loading up the cars with our belongings. Before I knew what was happening, we were back on the road again.

I couldn't understand what happened. I was absolutely dumbfounded and then I had a terrible thought. Maybe this was my new normal. Maybe I was destined to spend the rest of my life in the backseat of Bud's car. Other than a few hours in our room the night before, I'd never in all my dog years spent so much time traveling. Now, don't get me wrong: I was really quite comfortable. I had my blankets and pillows; Bud played tunes by Billy, Bruce, Bob, and even Peter, Paul and Mary; I was with my people; the snacks and treats were plentiful; and I'd thoroughly enjoyed a perfectly prepared charbroiled cheddar cheeseburger and fries the night before.

And so, Bud drove, Bunny drove, and I dozed on and off for the next umpteen hours. I recall passing signs welcoming us to Indiana and Illinois. These states greeted us with open paws, and yet we just kept going. When we passed over the Mississippi River into Missouri – well, I was beyond flabbergasted. Not only was I flabbergasted, but I was flummoxed as well. Then I had a wonderful thought. I remembered watching an entire TV program about a specific type of barbeque prepared in St. Louis. My only hope, after spending so much time in the car, was that we'd find one of the restaurants featured in that program. But – no – they kept going until we finally stopped for the night and instead of carefully prepared barbequed chicken, we shared dinner from a place where the food came wrapped in a soggy paper wrapper. Trust me when I tell you how disappointed I was to have been so close to those restaurants from the TV program, and yet so incredibly far away.

That night we moved into another building that looked strangely like the place we'd stayed the night before. The only difference was the décor in the lobby. The entire experience reminded me of an episode from one of those old science fictions shows. When you think about the fact that we'd spent the entire day traveling only to stay in an identical room as the previous night – well what's a dog to think. And then we were back in the car again the next morning.

To say this was all getting a bit redundant would be a gross understatement. And then it happened: we entered Kansas, the Sunflower State, the Wheat State, the Jayhawker State, the OMG this road is unbelievably straight and flat and I'm in the Looking for Toto State. At this point, I was just about ready to jump out of my fur coat altogether. I needed a break. I needed a rest from so much driving. I needed to go home. I'll never forget our lunch break in Kansas. It was just off the highway and down what looked like a dirt road. Yes: it was another in a long series of chain burger joints, adjacent to a dilapidated church with a tornado shelter sign out front.

And yes, that night we moved back in to another identical building. I was now terrified. We'd been on the road for what seemed like forever, and yet we kept returning to identical places to sleep every night. On the other paw, there were three colossal differences on our third night. The first was I felt light headed, dizzy, and dopey. It was as if someone had slipped a Mickey into my water dish when I wasn't looking. The second difference was that we were now in Colorado, just outside of Denver, which may explain my lightheadedness. (I'd heard that the altitude in the Centennial State can make some feel a bit off kilter.) The third difference was that in spite of my feelings of vertigo, there was a genuine restaurant next door to our place. Although they openly discriminated against four-legged patrons, we still ordered dinner there and ate it back in our room. Spaghetti and meatballs never tasted so good as it did that night. Sure, I was a bit queasy from the altitude, but I still managed to enjoy my dinner.

The next day was incredible. Obviously, we were back on the road again, but I was doggone sure we weren't in Kansas anymore. Almost as soon as we left our place near Denver, it seemed as if we drove straight into the heavens. I must admit that as sick and tired as I was of being stuck in the back seat of the car, traveling through the Rockies was remarkable. I doggedly watched Bud's driving, not because he's unsafe behind the wheel, but because he'd never driven on such a road before.

The mountain peaks, the sheer cliffs, the majestic views, were really quite distracting and he needed to pay extra close attention to road in front of him. Remaining alert was his job. Acting as one of those guard dog types to be sure he remained alert, well that was my job – and it was really rather stressful. I kept seeing signs with blinking lights warning of steep grades and sharp curves, so as we traveled straight into the mountains through white tiled tunnels with bright white fluorescent lights on either side, I honestly thought that perhaps we'd crashed and we were on the brink of entering the big doggy door in the sky. Needless to say, we exited the tunnel and were back in the middle of majestic magnificence. And so, our journey through the Colorado Rockies was incredible – but what came next was almost as breathtaking.

At some point after entering Utah, Bunny and Bud made a decision to exit the highway and travel down a narrow two-lane road along the Colorado River. We even stopped at a pull-off so I could dip my paw in its clear waters. Now I'm not one to go swimming or even wading, but on this occasion, I made an exception. When you think about it, how many dogs from The Bronx have such an opportunity. I only wish those punks from the streets could have seen me. After a short riverside break, we continued along the same road until we finally reached a place called Moab. Yes – the views and the vistas were quite a vision, but what came next was something I'd all but given up hope of encountering on this never-ending expedition.

We pulled into a restaurant that openly appreciated four-legged patrons who weren't officially educated as service-dogs. The patio/deck was clearly welcoming and the waitstaff even provided me with a delicious bowl of water from the soda fountain: minus the bubbles, minus the soda, and minus the ice.

It was a relief to finally be waited on like any other customer and not be forced to eat food out of a cellulous wrapper or a plastic box. This goes to show that you shouldn't give up hope. It took a gazillion days in the car, but we finally found a dining establishment that welcomed my pack – and me. The food was outstanding: turkey and gravy, mashed potatoes, and carrots. Was it at all possible that we'd schlepped from New York State to Utah simply to find this very place? Had all the hours I'd logged in the backseat been worth the trouble, and my bewilderment about determining our ultimate mission – which I now knew was this Thanksgiving-like dinner – worth it? The answers were absolutely and unfortunately: no.

After we all enjoyed our delicious al fresco dining experience, we loaded back into the cars and traveled even further west. This had to be it: this was now my life. I had no home. I had no yard. I had no privacy. Even though I'd actually enjoyed that day's excursion, I was now resolved that the rest of my days would be spent in Bud's backseat, while my nights would be spent in that same hotel room, only this one was somewhere in the Beehive State. It was sad, but true.

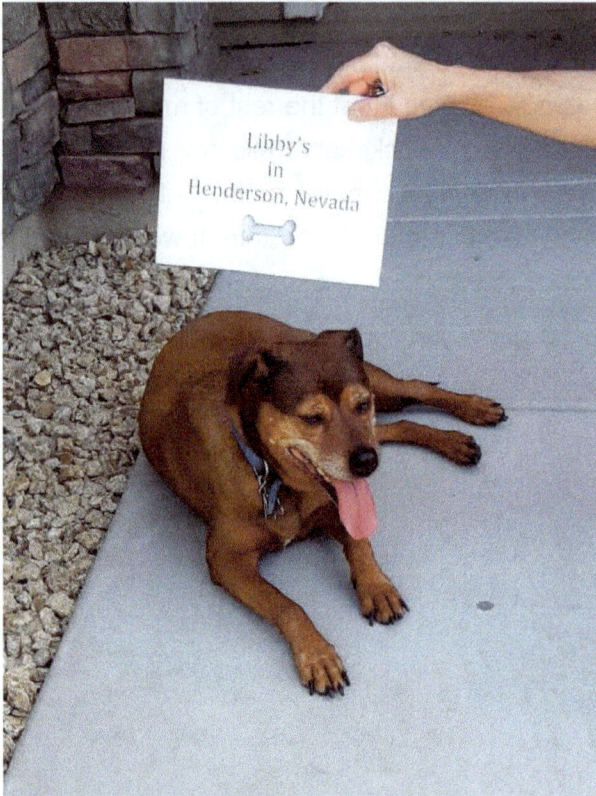

Libby's
in
Henderson, Nevada

The next morning, something just felt different. I couldn't quite put my paw on what it was, but something was definitely happening. We were up and out early, back in the cars, and I could sense some sort of excitement I hadn't felt on previous days. My only hope was that we'd return to that same place in Moab for dinner. Well, imagine my surprise when I saw the sign welcoming us to Nevada. So much for returning to my new favorite restaurant. Bunny and Bud were busy chatting on their radios – much more so than any of the previous days.

We drove south through the city of Las Vegas. I could see Fremont Street and Las Vegas Boulevard, but they never pulled over. I was actually hoping to stop and shoot craps or play the slots, but they just kept going. It all seemed so close, and yet so far away. A few minutes later they entered a place called Henderson. Okay: big deal, who cares? They parked our cars in front of a house and we all walked inside. The place was nice enough, but it was far too new for my taste.

When they weren't looking, I ran back to Bud's car and hopped in the backseat. The place they were visiting didn't seem overly exciting, I didn't smell anything cooking, and to be honest, it all looked rather boring. Consequently, I made an executive decision to simply wait in the car. After all, we'd surely be pulling out soon enough. I didn't know it then, but this was it. We'd reached the end of the line, our final destination, our terminus.

They called me back in from the car and then I started exploring the insides of this new house. I started to recognize aromas from days gone by: the sweet smells of my own tush on our sofa, our bed from back in New York, and best of all my old quilt, the one that had once belonged to Bunny and Bud. I was befuddled, dumbfounded, and perplexed to have practically moved into a car, traveled across the entire country for what seemed like a trillion days, only to find myself in Nevada with the same things I left back at home. Of course, I was genuinely comforted to inhale familiar scents. And so – this was our new house, our new town, our new State. We were home, but even though it was all new to me, I was still with my pack, the people I'd trained and grown to love, and we were all together.

Our move to the Nevada was unexpected, but now that I've been in my new home for several years, I've become acclimated to my new surroundings. In fact, I like to tell others that I retired to the southwest. I often meet other retired dogs when I'm walking in local parks, and many of them also relocated from cold weather climates. We share stories of relieving ourselves in the midst of a snowstorm or attempts to remain steady on icy pavement. Fortunately for me and my new friends, those times are just a distant memory. Sure, it gets hot in the summer, but the sun's warmth feels great on my arthritic hips and back. As long as I stay well hydrated, I'm fine.

Review the checklist on the following page and ponder how you would respond to being schlepped cross-country.

1. **You're always up for a ride, but spending all day every day in the car is too much.**

Yes   _____

No   _____

Unsure   _____

If yes, you would have plottzed on this never-ending outing. After our first 15 minutes, I was ready to get out of the car. To survive, I recommend implementing a strict napping routine. As you dream of running, walking and sauntering, you'll sense your legs and paws moving back and forth. This will keep your blood flow intact.

If no, you must love to sit in one place for hours at a time. Be careful not to get a deep vein thrombosis or DVT. Movement is essential to your health. You're more likely to move in your sleep than sitting staring out the car window.

2. **You traveled all day, moved into an ideal place, only to repeat the process again.**

Please make it stop   _____

This is exciting   _____

Unsure   _____

If you want it to stop, I have bad news for you. This situation is largely out of your control. Think of it as that film grounddog day (yes, I know) and life keeps repeating over and over again.

If you think this is exciting, I recommend a period of self-reflection and perhaps some analysis.

3. **If you're stuck in the car, you know you'll be safe as long as your person is with you.**

Absolutely	_____
No	_____
Unsure	_____

If you responded absolutely, I'm in total agreement with you. At this point, I'm hopeful that you've developed a genuine attachment, a bond, a visceral understanding with your person and your entire pack. There's a mutual trust between you and there's no need to fear the future – even if it is rather repetitive.

If no, you need to ask yourself why there's a lack of trust between you, your person, and your pack. It's not their fault you were on the streets. They treat you like royalty and this is how you repay them? I feel very sorry for you.

Step Eleven: Growing Old

✓ **At the end of Step Eleven, you'll recognize what you likely already know. As the years pass, dogs and people get older.**

NOTE: Believe it or not, I've overheard callous observations about not being able to teach old dogs new tricks. This assumes that young dogs can and should learn tricks – which is also rather derogatory and offensive. I've never performed in a circus or any other kind of stage or side show and if I had, that would have been my choice and not anyone else's. It's beyond my comprehension as to why a normal, upstanding canine such as myself would need or want to learn any tricks in the first place. Be that as it may, I believe the essence of the adage implies that we all mature and age over time – both physically and emotionally.

The object of this lesson is to share some rather harsh truths about canine longevity and health. I've heard claims that most dogs only have a lifespan of six to fourteen calendar years. That's a significant range and it largely depends on their breeds and their DNA, as well as their specific BMI. These scientific studies generally don't account for dogs such as me – dogs who are the product of the passion between two distinct and dissimilar breeds in a Bronx stairwell. Also, it doesn't mean that we only exist as children or adolescents. By the time many of us are seven years old, we're referred to as middle age, or roughly in our late forties in human terms. Let's be blunt, that really sucks. Please understand that I don't claim to be a canine geneticist, researcher, or medical professional, so keep in mind that this lesson is based strictly on my own life experiences and first-hand knowledge living life as a dog.

When I was relatively young and living with my pack back in New York, I trained them to spend time off their leash, as long as we were all outdoors together. Once I realized they could be trusted not to run away from me, I used to run laps around the outside of our house. Seriously, can you believe that? I'd disembark from our front porch and then run solo laps across the front yard, around to the back, and stop for a cool refreshing beverage back where I started in front. No one could keep up with me. It was absolutely exhilarating. For a short while, I considered entering some athletic competitions but thought better of it when I realized I'd need to watch my caloric intake more closely. Sometimes I'd run laps with my pals Echo, Blizzard, and Chilly. Once in a while we'd even make friendly wagers on who'd come in first. We also enjoyed a game called Leap Dog. It's similar to leap frog, only with – well – you know, dogs. That's when we were all young, healthy, and full of energy. I wish I could relive those times, but instead I simply dream about the days when my energy was limitless.

I'd almost forgotten to share this story which clearly demonstrates my athleticism back in the day. Amazingly, I used to jump up on our dining room table and help myself to whatever happened to be there.

This ranged from snatching a roll of mint-flavored antacids (which were really rather tasty) to just sorting through whatever papers happened to be there. Now, I'm not talking about standing up on my back paws to reach something from the kitchen counter, such as the peach pie. No – I mean it was like an Olympic pole vaulter only without the pole. I could go from a standing position next to the table and jump so all four paws were firmly planted on the table top. The first time I attempted this skill, I wasn't entirely successful but after a bit of practice, I became doggone good at this.

Regrettably as the years have progressed, my overall athleticism has waned. Things such as jumping up on the bed, which was once no problem, is now virtually impossible. Instead of running sprints, I'm often content to lay on the couch to watch the shopping channel and old movies (preferably ones where the lead has four legs, a tail, and a deep sexy bark). Hey – I'm an old woman on the outside, but inside I'm still full of passion.

I adopted Bunny and Bud over fourteen years ago and, from what I recall, at that point I was about two years old. So, let's face it, I'm not old – I'm actually rather elderly. During the past decade and a half, my people have also aged and yet for some bizarre biological reason it seems I've gotten so much older than they have during the same period. It's a peculiar phenomenon, but while they've aged years and months, I feel as if I've aged multiple decades.

While getting old isn't something I thought I'd enjoy, there are incredible benefits to being as physically mature as I am now. Yes, I'm always running to the doctor's office for pokes, pricks, and prescription refills, but I'm also living a pretty cushy life right now. Perhaps it's because of the time I spent wandering the streets in my youth, but for the most part I'm in pretty good shape. I still maintain a strict exercise routine that would put most dogs half my age to shame.

Bud and I endeavor to take at least three lengthy walks every day. As you learned in the previous lesson, I now reside in southern Nevada which means there's no need to concern myself with snow and ice – so we walk throughout the entire year. These aren't slow strolls. No, these are honest to goodness walks in various parks located near our home. The physical exercise is obviously the primary goal of these excursions, but there's a side benefit as well. On the vast majority of our outings we encounter other dogs, and I must say I've had more than a few adolescent muscular males try to take a whiff of my tail. At my age, it's rather flattering that I can still retrieve Retrievers and make the boldest Sheep Dog feel at least somewhat sheepish.

Another benefit to my advanced years is that I've managed to convince Bunny that I can't dine without her assistance. I'm not sure if she's really as hoodwinked as she behaves, but I have her eating right out of my paw. Obviously since we've been together many years, I've had ample opportunity to mold her behavior to meet my needs. If you're as fortunate as I am, you also have a person who is remarkably pliable, educable, and gullible. You may be astounded to learn that I've managed to convince her that, for the most part, I'll only eat food that's literally served out of the palm of her paw – or rather hand.

And so, I play this little mind game with her and since she's so devoted to serving me, she loses the game every single time – breakfast, lunch, and dinner. This is how it works. It's really rather a simple and unsophisticated charade we play. She dishes out my food, sets it down in front of me, I walk away, she picks up the dish, walks or crawls to where I've gone, and then she scoops the food into her hand and I eat every last bite. That's it in a nutshell. Yes, there are a few caveats.

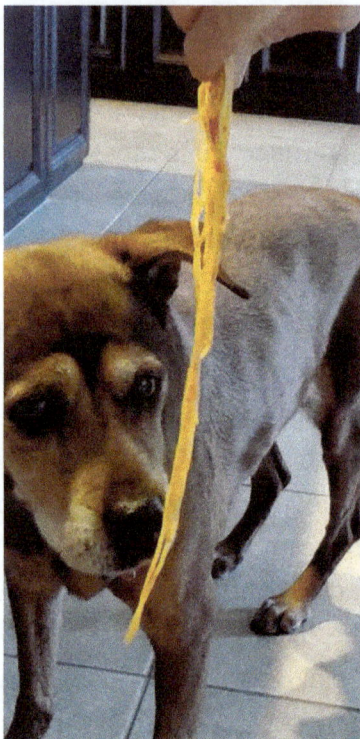

First, you may need to control your urge to eat the food as presented – aka dining unassisted. She may serve a sizzling rib steak or hamburger right off the grill, or a freshly boned rotisserie chicken. Don't be lulled into wolfing down such delicacies without making her play the game. The little farce or act we engage in actually gives her a sense of purpose – a sense of belonging to the pack. After all she's done for you, you owe it to her to play the game.

Second, she'll likely try to slip some sort of medication into your food while feeding you. It may be a pill or some horrid-tasting tonic. Trust me: there's no better way to spoil a perfectly seared piece of salmon than to serve it on top of brown goopy medicine. On the other hand, you need to trust your person not to poison you. Whatever they're trying to get you to swallow is likely for your own health and wellbeing. Just hold your nose, close your eyes, down the goop, and then take a long swig of spring water. Seriously – it'll help.

Finally, don't be shy about asking for seconds. At this stage of life, why not enjoy. When you realize I'm close to ninety years old in human chronological years, I think I'm entitled to eat whatever and whenever I please. Now some dogs and/or people may disagree with this premise, but I honestly don't care.

Still another benefit to growing old and living where we now live is the fact that Bud and I bought a convertible. Well actually, Bud and Bunny bought the car but I undeniably love cruising around town with my man while we leave Bunny at home to prepare meals for us. He puts down the roof, I don my paisley bandana, and away we go. I feel like a movie star in one of those old films from the fifties.

You should see us with the wind blowing through my fur, my scarf flapping in the desert breeze, and Bud cranking the tunes on the radio: it's like living the dream baby. He leans over, puts his arm around me, kisses me, and I ask you, what more could an old dog like me want out of life? On occasion Bunny suggests chaperoning our outings, but we're usually able to convince her that we need our privacy and that three's really a crowd, especially in a convertible.

And so as you can tell, being a canine of advanced years isn't the worst thing in the world. In fact, it can actually be pretty great. Regrettably, not all dogs live to the age I am right now, and I'm truly sorry for that. That fact is far too sad and unfair to even think about, for their people and for them. On the other hand, this is my story and my life lessons and this is all I know. I'm well aware that one day I'll cross what many believe to be a rainbow bridge – to a special place were dogs of all breeds, shapes, and sizes can play and lounge in the sun together. It sounds wonderful, although I know I'll miss my Bunny and Bud and they'll miss me when that day comes. In the meantime, we cherish each day we have together.

Review the checklist on the following page and consider the following tips on growing old.

1. **Maintaining an exercise regime helps to keep old dogs from behaving like old dogs.**

Yes   _____
No   _____
Unsure   _____

If yes, you're a smart pup. You may not feel like exercising, but you understand its importance both physically and mentally. The physical part is obvious, but on the mental or emotional side, perhaps you use these opportunities to rendezvous with a snazzy French Poodle, or a Chinese Shar-pei and its exquisite blue/black tongue.

If no, you need to get out of the house and live a little. You don't need to run a marathon to get your respiration and heartrate going. There's an entire world outside just waiting for your big shnozz to sniff.

2. **Old dogs can and should teach their people new tricks.**

Yes   _____
No   _____
Unsure   _____

If yes, I agree with you entirely. I taught Bunny to feed me from her paw, and she now performs this trick without any prompting or cues. It took a number of training sessions, but she now functions on a sort of autopilot at meal times, and what's more is she seems to enjoy this time together.

If no, don't give up on your person. Unless they are unwilling and/or unable to comprehend simple instructions, they should be able to learn new skills. Depending on their age and disposition it may take longer to teach them. The key is to be patient, understanding, and give them a little treat when they perform well.

3. <u>You believe it is your role to continue your work to guide your people in their old age.</u>

Yes   _____

No   _____

Unsure   _____

If yes, I admire and applaud your commitment. Old people, like old dogs, deserve to be loved and cared for in their old age. Your person would never dump you just because you're on the other side of middle aged. The same is true for people. You may need to be a little bit more patient as your person ages, but loving and guiding your person, your pack is a lifetime responsibility.

If no, what kind of dog are you? I mean – really. Don't you have any sense of loyalty or love for your pack or your people? They opened their home to you, loved you, cared for you, and this is how you repay them?

Lesson Summaries

I trust you've read through the preceding eleven lessons and completed the corresponding self-evaluations. Each of these steps and modules were designed with you in mind: my canine friends. As you go forth into the world or stop to reassess your future, I urge you to remember the following lessons, examples, and thought-provoking case studies: follow your dream; choose your person carefully; start the training process immediately; don't be shy – take the next step; always remember: your family is your pack; bad things may happen to good dogs; care for your personal hygiene; vacationing away from your pack; caring for your pack; retirement and moving west; and growing old.

Please understand that learning life's lessons isn't easy for anyone and there's no "one size fits all" response to all situations. There are far too many variations to address in one simple guide, so please keep in mind that this book was written from my unique perspective – the harmonious blend between a Rhodesian Ridgeback and a Pitbull, as well as that of a queen. Many believe I'm an incredibly lucky dog to have been adopted by people who respect, revere, and care for me, and I whole heartily agree with them.

As you continue to absorb the lessons in this book, I only ask that you never forget that your breed, size, socioeconomic status, culture, and geographic circumstances are just a few factors which will likely impact the life style you and your pack live. Even so, I sincerely wish such a thought-provoking guidance document had been available for me when I was still a young pup. Never forget that you have no choice but to navigate a world filled with people. Possessing the emotional wherewithal to live with an entirely different species is an essential skill for dogs. I don't think most humans fully comprehend the significance of this fact. They should consider how they would feel being forced to live as the only person in a house full of Pugs, Pomeranians, or Papillons. I suppose what I'm saying, is that mutual respect, understanding, and patience is the key to life.

Regrettably, many dogs aren't as fortunate as you or me. I include you in the same category as me because I'm guessing that someone, likely a human, cared enough to buy this book for you. This may come as a shock, but there are far too many people in the world who treat their dogs as second or even third-class beings – and worse. Dogs are physically and emotionally bullied and abused. They're not treated with respect, or as if they're individuals with feelings, wants, and needs. You know as much as I do, that we have emotions and are far more sensitive than many humans.

After reading, absorbing, and contemplating this book, I encourage you and your pack to adopt a loving dog from a local shelter or rescue organization. If they're not able to open your home to a dog, encourage them to donate their time and/or money to organizations dedicated to helping dogs follow their dreams. It was through the generosity of such a group called Peppertree Rescue[3], that I was united with Bunny and Bud. Likewise, my predecessor in the pack, Snowball, was cared for by a shelter operated by the Mohawk-Hudson Humane Society[4]. There are many similar organizations around the country. Never forget that there are countless companions just waiting for someone to take a chance on them.

---

[3] http://peppertree.org/

[4] https://mohawkhumane.org/

And now – one final checklist.

Adopting your person is a lifetime commitment.

Yes   _____

No   _____

Unsure   _____

If yes, you understand that when a dog adopts their person, it isn't as a fleeting fancy or a novel and cutesy holiday or birthday gift. As smug as you may think I am, in truth I really need my people. I depend on them for my physical and emotional security, as well as delicious treats.

I'm genuinely sorry you feel this way. You may have been the victim of a revolving door at the local penitentiary – or worse. Just be patient. I'm hopeful the right person is just waiting for you to bring them into your life.

Shelter dogs are scary. Someone dumped them there because they can't be trusted.

Yes   _____

NO   _____

Unsure   _____

If yes, I'm not sure what side of the kibble bowl you were brought up on, but that couldn't be farther from the truth. I'm a prime example that incredibly intelligent and loving dogs sometimes end up in the big house through no fault of their own. Without people like Bunny and Bud who are smart enough and brave enough to look beyond the bars, beyond a dog's rap sheet, millions more dogs would be homeless, loveless, and destitute.

If no, you must have read my book. Obviously not every dog in the hoosegow is angel, but they're the exception and not the rule. As you likely know, sometimes people simply can't keep their canine companions – whether due to illness, financial issues, or even *their* incarceration! Don't hold it against the dog. I can't think of any dog who'd rather be in the clink instead of in a loving home.

People enrich dog's lives.

Yes   _____
No   _____
Unsure   _____

If yes, you're well aware of the fact that Bunny and Bud have enriched my life. They've shown me a world beyond The Bronx. They treat me with respect, and as a companion. Most of all, they treat me like a queen.

If no, reread this book.

Portrait of Libby by Renee Engel Krosner Slone

Other novels, novellas and short story collections available from
Stairwell Books

For further information please contact rose@stairwellbooks.com
www.stairwellbooks.co.uk
@stairwellbooks